Positive Thinking

Unlock the Power of Your Mind and Transform Your Life with Positive Thinking: A Comprehensive Guide to Overcoming Negative Thoughts, Boosting Self-Confidence, and Achieving Your Dreams!

Lance P. Richards

I0625372

Positive Thinking - Unlock the Power of Your Mind and Transform Your Life with Positive Thinking: A Comprehensive Guide to Overcoming Negative Thoughts, Boosting Self-Confidence, and Achieving Your Dreams!

Table of Contents

01: Introduction: Understanding the Power of Positive Thinking

Positive thinking is a concept that has gained popularity over the years, and for good reason. It is a powerful tool that can transform one's life by changing their mindset and outlook. Positive thinking involves focusing on the positive aspects of life, rather than dwelling on the negative. It is a state of mind that can lead to greater happiness, success, and overall well-being.

The power of positive thinking lies in the way it can affect a person's thoughts, emotions, and actions. When a person thinks positively, they are more likely to have positive emotions and take positive actions. This can lead to greater success in all areas of life, including career, relationships, and personal growth.

The opposite of positive thinking is negative thinking, which can lead to negative emotions and actions. Negative thinking can limit a person's potential and prevent them from achieving their goals. It can also lead to stress, anxiety, and depression.

The good news is that positive thinking can be learned and

practiced. It is a skill that can be developed over time with the right mindset and tools. The first step to harnessing the power of positive thinking is to understand the concept and its benefits.

Benefits of Positive Thinking

There are numerous benefits to adopting a positive thinking mindset. Some of the most notable benefits include:

– Increased Happiness: Positive thinking can lead to greater feelings of happiness and contentment. When a person focuses on the positive aspects of their life, they are more likely to feel grateful and satisfied with what they have.

– Improved Health: Research has shown that positive thinking can lead to improved physical health. People who think positively are less likely to experience stress and are more likely to engage in healthy behaviors such as exercise and healthy eating.

– Increased Resilience: Positive thinking can increase a person's ability to bounce back from setbacks and challenges.

01: INTRODUCTION: UNDERSTANDING THE POWER OF POSITIVE THINKING

When a person has a positive outlook, they are more likely to see challenges as opportunities for growth and learning.

– Improved Relationships: Positive thinking can lead to improved relationships with others. When a person thinks positively, they are more likely to be kind, compassionate, and empathetic towards others.

– Increased Success: Positive thinking can lead to greater success in all areas of life, including career, relationships, and personal growth. When a person thinks positively, they are more likely to take positive actions that lead to success.

How to Develop a Positive Thinking Mindset

Developing a positive thinking mindset is a process that requires practice and patience. The following are some tips to help develop a positive thinking mindset:

– Practice Gratitude: One of the easiest ways to develop a positive thinking mindset is to practice gratitude. This involves focusing on the positive aspects of one's life and expressing gratitude for them.

– Surround Yourself with Positivity: Surrounding oneself

with positive people and positive influences can help to reinforce a positive mindset. This can include reading positive books, watching positive movies, and spending time with positive people.

– Focus on Solutions: Instead of dwelling on problems, focus on finding solutions. When a person has a positive mindset, they are more likely to approach problems with a solution-focused mindset.

– Practice Positive Self-Talk: The way a person talks to themselves can have a significant impact on their mindset. Practicing positive self-talk can help to reinforce a positive mindset.

– Visualize Success: Visualizing success can help to reinforce a positive mindset and increase the likelihood of success. When a person visualizes themselves achieving their goals, they are more likely to take positive actions that lead to success.

Positive thinking is a powerful tool that can transform a person's life. By adopting a positive mindset and focusing on the positive aspects of life, a person can increase their happiness, success, and overall well-being. Developing a positive thinking mindset takes time and effort, but the benefits are well worth it. By practicing gratitude, surrounding oneself with positivity, focusing on solutions, practicing positive self-talk, and visualizing success, a person can develop a more positive outlook on life.

It's important to note that positive thinking does not mean ignoring negative emotions or pretending that everything is perfect. Rather, it means acknowledging the negative aspects of life while focusing on the positive. It's about finding a balance between positivity and realism.

In this book, we will explore the power of positive thinking and provide a comprehensive guide to overcoming negative thoughts, boosting self-confidence, and achieving your dreams. Each chapter will focus on a specific aspect of positive thinking, providing practical tips and strategies for developing a more positive mindset.

We hope that this book will inspire and empower you to unlock the power of positive thinking and transform your life. Remember, positive thinking is a journey, not a destination. With consistent effort and practice, anyone can develop a more positive mindset and enjoy the many benefits that come with it.

02: The Science behind Positive Thinking

Positive thinking is not just a feel-good concept; there is scientific evidence that supports its benefits. Research has shown that positive thinking can have a profound impact on a person's mental and physical health, as well as their overall well-being. In this chapter, we will explore the science behind positive thinking and how it affects the brain and body.

– The Power of Neuroplasticity

The brain is a complex organ that is constantly changing and adapting. This ability of the brain to change is known as neuroplasticity. Neuroplasticity is the brain's ability to form new neural connections and pathways in response to experiences, thoughts, and emotions.

Research has shown that positive thinking can have a significant impact on neuroplasticity. When a person thinks positively, they are more likely to activate regions of the brain that are associated with positive emotions, such as the prefrontal cortex and the anterior cingulate cortex. These regions of the brain are involved in decision-making, attention, and emotional regulation.

On the other hand, negative thinking can have a negative impact on neuroplasticity. When a person thinks negatively, they are more likely to activate regions of the brain that are associated with stress, anxiety, and depression. These regions of the brain include the amygdala and the hippocampus, which are involved in the stress response and emotional regulation.

– The Impact of Positive Thinking on Health

Positive thinking has been shown to have numerous health benefits. One of the most significant benefits is its impact on the immune system. Research has shown that positive emotions can boost the immune system by increasing the production of immune cells and reducing inflammation in the body.

Positive thinking has also been shown to have a positive impact on cardiovascular health. Studies have found that people who think positively are less likely to develop heart disease and have a lower risk of stroke.

In addition to physical health, positive thinking can also

have a significant impact on mental health. Research has shown that positive thinking can reduce symptoms of anxiety and depression and improve overall mental well-being.

– The Impact of Negative Thinking on Health

Negative thinking, on the other hand, has been shown to have a negative impact on health. Research has shown that negative emotions, such as stress and anxiety, can weaken the immune system and increase the risk of developing chronic diseases.

Negative thinking can also have a negative impact on mental health. Studies have found that negative thinking can increase the risk of developing anxiety and depression and can worsen symptoms of these conditions.

Strategies for Developing a Positive Thinking Mindset

There are several strategies that a person can use to develop a more positive thinking mindset. Some of these strategies include:

– Practicing Gratitude: Focusing on the positive aspects of life and expressing gratitude for them can help to reinforce a positive mindset.

– Surrounding Oneself with Positivity: Surrounding oneself with positive people and positive influences can help to reinforce a positive mindset.

– Visualizing Success: Visualizing success can help to reinforce a positive mindset and increase the likelihood of success.

– Practicing Positive Self-Talk: The way a person talks to themselves can have a significant impact on their mindset. Practicing positive self-talk can help to reinforce a positive mindset.

– Focusing on Solutions: Instead of dwelling on problems, focusing on finding solutions can help to reinforce a positive mindset.

Positive thinking is not just a feel-good concept; there is scientific evidence that supports its benefits. Research has shown that positive thinking can have a profound impact on a person's mental and physical health, as well as their overall well-being. By understanding the science behind positive thinking and implementing strategies for developing a positive thinking mindset, anyone can enjoy the benefits of a more positive outlook on life.

03: Overcoming Negative Thoughts and Beliefs

Negative thoughts and beliefs can be a significant barrier to achieving a more positive mindset. These thoughts and beliefs can be deeply ingrained, often stemming from childhood experiences or negative life events. However, it's important to recognize that negative thoughts and beliefs can be overcome with consistent effort and practice.

In this chapter, we will explore strategies for identifying and overcoming negative thoughts and beliefs, as well as the benefits of doing so.

Identifying Negative Thoughts and Beliefs

The first step in overcoming negative thoughts and beliefs is to identify them. Negative thoughts and beliefs can be sneaky, often operating at a subconscious level. However, there are several common thought patterns and beliefs that are associated with negativity, such as:

– Catastrophizing: Assuming the worst-case scenario will happen

– All-or-nothing thinking: Seeing things in black and white

with no gray area

– Overgeneralization: Drawing broad conclusions based on limited evidence

– Personalization: Taking things personally, even when they have nothing to do with you

– Perfectionism: Expecting everything to be perfect and beating oneself up for mistakes

Once you have identified these thought patterns and beliefs, you can begin to challenge them.

Challenging Negative Thoughts and Beliefs

Challenging negative thoughts and beliefs can be a difficult process, but it's an essential step in overcoming them. One effective strategy for challenging negative thoughts and beliefs is cognitive restructuring. Cognitive restructuring involves identifying and challenging negative thoughts and beliefs, replacing them with more positive ones.

For example, if you find yourself catastrophizing a situation, you can challenge that thought by asking yourself, "Is this really the worst-case scenario?" and then replacing that thought with a more realistic one, such as "Even if the worst-case scenario happens, I have the skills and resources to handle it."

Another effective strategy for challenging negative thoughts and beliefs is mindfulness. Mindfulness involves being present in the moment and observing thoughts and emotions without judgment. This can help you to recognize negative thought patterns and beliefs and respond to them in a more constructive way.

Benefits of Overcoming Negative Thoughts and Beliefs

Overcoming negative thoughts and beliefs can have numerous benefits, including:

– Improved mood: Challenging negative thoughts and beliefs can help to reduce feelings of sadness and anxiety.

– Increased self-esteem: Replacing negative thoughts and beliefs with more positive ones can help to boost self-esteem.

– Improved relationships: Negative thoughts and beliefs

can impact how you interact with others. By overcoming them, you may find that your relationships improve.

– Greater resilience: Overcoming negative thoughts and beliefs can help to build resilience, making it easier to cope with challenges and setbacks.

Negative thoughts and beliefs can be a significant barrier to achieving a more positive mindset. However, by identifying and challenging these thoughts and beliefs, you can overcome them and enjoy the benefits of a more positive outlook on life. Remember, this is a process that takes time and effort, but with consistent practice, anyone can overcome negative thoughts and beliefs and achieve a more positive mindset.

It's important to note that overcoming negative thoughts and beliefs is not a one-time event, but rather an ongoing process. It requires consistent effort and practice, as well as the willingness to challenge negative thoughts and beliefs as they arise.

One key aspect to consider when working to overcome negative thoughts and beliefs is self-compassion. It's important to be kind and understanding with yourself throughout this process. Negative thoughts and beliefs can be deeply ingrained, and it's not always easy to overcome them. Remember that progress, not perfection, is the goal.

Another important aspect to consider is seeking professional help if needed. Sometimes negative thoughts and beliefs can be a sign of a larger mental health issue, such as depression or anxiety. In these cases, seeking professional help from a therapist or counselor can be incredibly beneficial.

In conclusion, overcoming negative thoughts and beliefs is an essential step in developing a more positive mindset. By identifying and challenging negative thought patterns and beliefs, and replacing them with more positive ones, anyone can enjoy the benefits of a more positive outlook on life. Remember to be kind and compassionate with yourself throughout this process, and seek professional help if needed. With consistent effort and practice, anyone can overcome negative thoughts and beliefs and achieve a more positive mindset.

04: Practicing Gratitude and Appreciation

Practicing gratitude and appreciation is an essential part of developing a positive mindset. It involves focusing on the good in our lives, rather than dwelling on the negative. This chapter will explore the benefits of practicing gratitude and appreciation, as well as strategies for incorporating these practices into your daily life.

Benefits of Practicing Gratitude and Appreciation

Practicing gratitude and appreciation has numerous benefits, both for our mental and physical health. Some of these benefits include:

– Improved mood: Focusing on the good in our lives can help to boost our mood and reduce feelings of sadness and anxiety.

– Increased resilience: Practicing gratitude and appreciation can help to build resilience, making it easier to cope with challenges and setbacks.

– Improved relationships: Expressing gratitude and appreciation can help to strengthen relationships and improve communication.

– Increased self-esteem: By focusing on the good in our lives, we can improve our self-esteem and feel more confident in ourselves.

– Improved physical health: Practicing gratitude and appreciation has been linked to improved physical health, including better sleep and decreased inflammation.

Strategies for Practicing Gratitude and Appreciation

There are many different ways to practice gratitude and appreciation, and it's important to find strategies that work for you. Here are some suggestions for incorporating these practices into your daily life:

– Keep a gratitude journal: Taking the time to write down things you're grateful for can help to focus your mind on the good in your life. Try to write down at least three things each day, no matter how small.

– Express gratitude to others: Take the time to express gratitude to the people in your life who have made a positive impact. This can be as simple as sending a thank-you note or verbalizing your appreciation.

– Practice mindfulness: Being present in the moment and paying attention to the world around us can help to cultivate a sense of gratitude and appreciation. Try to focus on the small moments of joy in your day-to-day life.

– Take a gratitude walk: Take a walk and focus on the things you're grateful for in your environment. This can be as simple as appreciating the beauty of nature or the architecture in your city.

– Start the day with gratitude: Begin your day by focusing on the things you're grateful for. This can help to set a positive tone for the rest of your day.

– Practice gratitude during meals: Take a moment before or during meals to express gratitude for the food you're about to eat and the people who made it possible.

Practicing gratitude and appreciation is an essential part of developing a positive mindset. By focusing on the good in our lives, we can improve our mood, build resilience, and improve our relationships. There are many different strategies for incorporating gratitude and appreciation into our daily lives, and it's important to find the practices that work best for us. Remember, practicing gratitude and appreciation is a process that takes time and effort, but with consistent practice, anyone can cultivate a more positive outlook on life.

It's important to note that practicing gratitude and appreciation doesn't mean ignoring or denying the challenges and struggles we face. It simply means shifting our focus to the positive aspects of our lives, rather than dwelling on the negative. By acknowledging and accepting both the good and the bad in our lives, we can cultivate a sense of balance and perspective.

One common obstacle to practicing gratitude and appreciation is the belief that we don't have anything to be grateful for. It's important to remember that there is always something to be grateful for, even in the most difficult circumstances. It can be helpful to start small, focusing on simple things like a good cup of coffee or a friendly conversation with a coworker.

Another common obstacle is the belief that expressing gratitude and appreciation is awkward or uncomfortable. It's important to remember that expressing gratitude is a gift to both ourselves and others. By taking the time to express our appreciation, we can strengthen our relationships and build a sense of connection with the people in our lives.

In conclusion, practicing gratitude and appreciation is a powerful tool for developing a positive mindset. By focusing on the good in our lives, we can improve our mood, build resilience, and improve our relationships. There are many different strategies for incorporating gratitude and appreciation into our daily lives, and it's important to find the practices that work best for us. With consistent effort and practice, anyone can cultivate a more positive outlook on life.

05: Developing a Positive Mindset

A positive mindset is the foundation for a happy and fulfilling life. It is the attitude of seeing the good in every situation, believing in ourselves and our abilities, and approaching life with optimism and hope. In this chapter, we'll explore the benefits of a positive mindset, as well as strategies for developing and maintaining one.

Benefits of a Positive Mindset

A positive mindset has numerous benefits for our mental and physical health, as well as our relationships and overall well-being. Some of these benefits include:

– Reduced stress and anxiety: A positive mindset can help to reduce stress and anxiety by shifting our focus away from negative thoughts and feelings.

– Improved resilience: A positive mindset can help us to bounce back from challenges and setbacks more quickly and effectively.

– Better physical health: A positive mindset has been linked to better physical health, including a stronger immune system and lower risk of chronic disease.

– Improved relationships: A positive mindset can improve our relationships by making us more open, empathetic, and approachable.

– Increased happiness and fulfillment: A positive mindset can help us to feel happier and more fulfilled in our lives, by allowing us to focus on the good and appreciate what we have.

Strategies for Developing a Positive Mindset

– Practice gratitude and appreciation: As discussed in the previous chapter, practicing gratitude and appreciation is an important part of developing a positive mindset. By focusing on the good in our lives, we can cultivate a sense of optimism and hope.

– Reframe negative thoughts: Whenever you find yourself thinking negatively, try to reframe those thoughts in a more positive light. For example, instead of thinking "I'll never be able to do this," try thinking "I may not be able to do it yet, but with practice, I can improve."

– Focus on solutions, not problems: Rather than dwelling on problems or obstacles, focus on finding solutions and taking action to overcome them.

– Surround yourself with positivity: Surround yourself with positive people, messages, and environments. This can help to reinforce a positive mindset and make it easier to maintain.

– Practice self-compassion: Be kind and compassionate to yourself, even when things don't go as planned. Remember that everyone makes mistakes and that failure is a natural part of the learning process.

– Practice mindfulness: Mindfulness involves being present in the moment and paying attention to your thoughts and feelings without judgment. By practicing mindfulness, you can become more aware of your thought patterns and learn to shift them in a more positive direction.

– Visualize success: Visualize yourself achieving your goals and living the life you want. This can help to build confidence and motivation, and make it easier to stay positive and focused.

Developing a positive mindset is an ongoing process that requires effort and commitment. By practicing gratitude and appreciation, reframing negative thoughts, focusing on solutions, surrounding yourself with positivity, practicing self-compassion, practicing mindfulness, and visualizing success, you can cultivate a more positive outlook on life. Remember, a positive mindset is not about denying or ignoring the challenges and struggles in life, but rather about approaching them with optimism, hope, and a willingness to learn and grow.

It's important to note that developing a positive mindset doesn't happen overnight, and it can take time and effort to overcome negative thought patterns and beliefs. It's also important to be patient with yourself and understand that setbacks and challenges are a natural part of the process.

One common challenge people face when trying to develop a positive mindset is negative self-talk. Negative self-talk is the inner dialogue we have with ourselves, which can be critical and self-defeating. Examples of negative self-talk include "I'm not good enough," "I'll never be successful," or "I always mess things up." These thoughts can be deeply ingrained and can hold us back from reaching our full potential.

To overcome negative self-talk, it's important to identify and challenge those negative thoughts. One way to do this is to ask yourself whether those thoughts are based on facts or assumptions. For example, if you think "I'm not good enough," ask yourself what evidence there is to support that belief. Is it a fact, or is it just an assumption based on your own fears and insecurities?

Another strategy for overcoming negative self-talk is to re-frame those thoughts in a more positive light. For example, if you think "I always mess things up," try reframing that thought as "I may have made mistakes in the past, but I can learn from them and do better in the future."

It's also important to practice self-compassion and kindness towards yourself. Treat yourself with the same kindness and understanding that you would offer to a good friend. Remember that making mistakes and facing challenges is a natural part of the learning and growth process, and that it's okay to not have everything figured out.

In addition to addressing negative self-talk, it's important to focus on positive affirmations and beliefs. Affirmations are positive statements that can help to reprogram our subconscious mind and reinforce positive beliefs about ourselves and our abilities. Examples of affirmations include "I am capable," "I am worthy of love and respect," or "I am confident in my abilities."

Finally, it's important to practice gratitude and appreciation on a daily basis. By focusing on the good in our lives, we can cultivate a sense of optimism and hope, and shift our focus away from negative thoughts and feelings.

In conclusion, developing a positive mindset is a powerful tool for transforming our lives and achieving our goals. By challenging negative thoughts and beliefs, practicing self-compassion and kindness, focusing on positive affirmations and beliefs, and practicing gratitude and appreciation, we can cultivate a more positive outlook on life and overcome the challenges and setbacks that we encounter along the way. Remember, the power to change our thoughts and beliefs lies within us, and with commitment and effort, we can unlock the full potential of our minds and transform our lives for the better.

06: Building Self-Confidence and Self-Esteem

Self-confidence and self-esteem are essential components of a positive mindset and are critical for achieving our goals and living fulfilling lives. While self-confidence and self-esteem are often used interchangeably, they are distinct concepts.

Self-esteem refers to our overall evaluation of ourselves, including our beliefs about our worthiness, value, and capabilities. In contrast, self-confidence refers to our belief in our abilities to accomplish specific tasks or goals.

Low self-esteem and self-confidence can result in feelings of insecurity, inadequacy, and self-doubt. These negative feelings can hold us back from taking risks, pursuing our goals, and living fulfilling lives. However, there are several strategies that we can use to build self-confidence and self-esteem.

One of the most effective ways to build self-confidence and self-esteem is to set achievable goals and work towards them. Accomplishing goals, no matter how small, can help us build confidence in our abilities and reinforce positive beliefs about ourselves. It's important to set realistic goals and break them down into smaller, manageable steps. This can help us avoid feeling overwhelmed and increase our chances of success.

Another strategy for building self-confidence and self-esteem is to practice self-care. This includes taking care of our physical health, such as getting enough sleep, eating a healthy diet, and exercising regularly. It also includes taking care of our emotional well-being by engaging in activities that bring us joy, connecting with supportive people, and taking time for ourselves to recharge and relax.

It's also important to practice self-compassion and treat ourselves with kindness and understanding. This includes acknowledging and accepting our imperfections and mistakes, rather than being overly self-critical or judgmental. By treating ourselves with kindness and compassion, we can build a stronger sense of self-worth and self-esteem.

Another effective strategy for building self-confidence and self-esteem is to challenge negative self-talk and beliefs. As discussed earlier, negative self-talk can be a significant barrier to building self-confidence and self-esteem. By identifying and challenging those negative thoughts and beliefs, we can replace them with more positive and empowering beliefs about ourselves and our abilities.

Finally, it's important to surround ourselves with supportive and positive people who encourage and believe in us. Having a supportive network can help us build confidence in our abilities and reinforce positive beliefs about ourselves.

In conclusion, building self-confidence and self-esteem is a critical component of a positive mindset and is essential for achieving our goals and living fulfilling lives. By setting achievable goals, practicing self-care, treating ourselves with compassion and kindness, challenging negative self-talk, and surrounding ourselves with supportive people, we can build self-confidence and self-esteem and unlock our full potential. Remember, building self-confidence and self-esteem is a journey, and it takes time and effort, but with commitment and perseverance, we can transform our lives for the better.

In addition to the strategies outlined above, there are other techniques that we can use to build self-confidence and self-esteem. These techniques include visualization, affirmations, and focusing on our strengths.

Visualization involves mentally picturing ourselves succeeding in a particular situation or accomplishing a specific goal. By visualizing ourselves succeeding, we can build confidence in our abilities and increase our chances of success.

Affirmations involve repeating positive statements about ourselves, such as "I am capable," "I am worthy," and "I am confident." By repeating these affirmations regularly, we can build positive beliefs about ourselves and increase our self-esteem.

Focusing on our strengths involves identifying our unique skills, talents, and qualities and recognizing how they contribute to our success. By focusing on our strengths, we can build confidence in our abilities and increase our self-esteem.

It's important to note that building self-confidence and self-esteem is not about being perfect or never experiencing self-doubt. Everyone experiences moments of self-doubt, and it's a natural part of the human experience. However, by practicing the strategies outlined above, we can learn to manage those feelings of self-doubt and build a stronger sense of self-confidence and self-esteem.

In summary, building self-confidence and self-esteem is a critical aspect of a positive mindset and is essential for achieving our goals and living fulfilling lives. By setting achievable goals, practicing self-care, treating ourselves with compassion and kindness, challenging negative self-talk, visualizing success, using affirmations, and focusing on our strengths, we can build self-confidence and self-esteem and unlock our full potential. Remember, building self-confidence and self-esteem is a journey, and it takes time and effort, but with commitment and perseverance, we can transform our lives for the better.

07: The Role of Visualization in Positive Thinking

Visualization is a powerful tool that can help us achieve our goals, build self-confidence, and maintain a positive mindset. It involves mentally picturing ourselves succeeding in a particular situation or accomplishing a specific goal. By visualizing ourselves succeeding, we can build confidence in our abilities and increase our chances of success.

The process of visualization involves creating a mental image of what we want to achieve. This image can be as detailed as we like, including sights, sounds, smells, and emotions. The more vivid and realistic the image, the more effective the visualization will be.

Visualization works because our brain does not distinguish between a real experience and an imagined one. When we visualize ourselves succeeding, our brain registers it as a real experience, and we experience the same feelings of accomplishment and confidence as if we had actually succeeded.

One of the most powerful aspects of visualization is that it can help us overcome our fears and self-doubt. By visualizing ourselves succeeding in situations that we find challenging or intimidating, we can build confidence in our abilities and reduce our anxiety.

For example, if we are nervous about giving a presentation at work, we can visualize ourselves delivering the presentation with confidence and receiving positive feedback from our colleagues. By repeatedly visualizing this scenario, we can build our confidence and reduce our anxiety.

Visualization can also be used to help us achieve our goals. By visualizing ourselves achieving our goals, we can build motivation and focus our attention on what we want to achieve. This can help us stay committed to our goals and overcome obstacles that may arise along the way.

To get the most out of visualization, it's important to practice regularly and be consistent. We can set aside time each day to visualize our goals and success, or we can incorporate visualization into our daily routine, such as visualizing ourselves succeeding before we go to bed at night or before we start our day in the morning.

It's also important to use visualization in conjunction with other positive thinking strategies, such as setting achievable goals, practicing self-care, challenging negative self-talk, and focusing on our strengths. By using these strategies together, we can build a strong foundation for a positive mindset and increase our chances of success.

In summary, visualization is a powerful tool that can help us achieve our goals, build self-confidence, and maintain a positive mindset. By creating vivid mental images of our success and repeatedly visualizing them, we can build our confidence, reduce our anxiety, and stay focused on our goals. With practice and consistency, visualization can be a valuable addition to our positive thinking toolbox.

There are several techniques and approaches that we can use to make our visualizations more effective. Here are a few tips to help you get started:

– Be specific: The more specific you can make your visualization, the more effective it will be. For example, instead of simply visualizing yourself winning a race, visualize yourself crossing the finish line in first place, feeling the rush of adrenaline and the sense of accomplishment.

– Use all of your senses: The more senses you can engage in your visualization, the more realistic it will feel. Try to imagine the sights, sounds, smells, and even the physical sensations associated with your goal or success.

– Practice regularly: Like any skill, visualization takes practice to master. Set aside time each day to practice your visualization, and be consistent in your approach.

– Use positive language: When visualizing your success, use positive language to describe what you see and feel. Instead of thinking "I don't want to fail," think "I am succeeding and achieving my goals."

– Believe in yourself: Visualization is most effective when we truly believe that we can achieve our goals. If you find yourself struggling with self-doubt or negative thoughts, take the time to address those issues before you begin your visualization practice.

In addition to these tips, it's also important to be patient and persistent. Visualization is not a quick fix or a one-time solution. It's a process that takes time and effort to develop, but the results can be truly transformative.

07: THE ROLE OF VISUALIZATION IN POSITIVE THINKING

By incorporating visualization into our positive thinking practice, we can build our self-confidence, achieve our goals, and maintain a positive mindset even in the face of adversity. So take some time to explore the power of visualization, and see how it can help you unlock your full potential and transform your life.

08: Affirmations and Their Power

Affirmations are a powerful tool for creating positive change in our lives. They are short, positive statements that are designed to help us reprogram our subconscious mind and shift our thoughts and beliefs in a more positive direction. By repeating affirmations regularly, we can replace negative self-talk with positive self-talk, and build our confidence, self-esteem, and overall sense of well-being.

Here are some ways in which affirmations can help transform our lives:

– Affirmations help us focus on the positive: By repeating positive statements about ourselves and our lives, we shift our focus away from negative thoughts and beliefs, and instead focus on the good things that we want to create in our lives.

– Affirmations build our self-confidence: When we repeat affirmations that are focused on our strengths, abilities, and positive qualities, we build our confidence and develop a more positive self-image.

– Affirmations help us overcome negative self-talk: Many of us have a tendency to engage in negative self-talk, criticizing ourselves for our mistakes and flaws. Affirmations help us to replace that negative self-talk with positive statements that affirm our worth and potential.

– Affirmations can help us achieve our goals: By setting goals and using affirmations to support those goals, we can focus our attention and energy on what we want to achieve, and increase our chances of success.

– Affirmations can improve our overall well-being: When we focus on positive thoughts and beliefs, we reduce our stress levels and improve our overall sense of well-being. Affirmations can help us to cultivate a more positive mind-set, which can lead to greater happiness and fulfillment in all areas of our lives.

To get the most out of affirmations, it's important to use them consistently and with intention. Here are some tips for creating and using affirmations:

– Be specific: Create affirmations that are focused on your specific goals or areas of your life that you want to improve. For example, instead of a general affirmation like "I am happy," try a more specific affirmation like "I am attracting positive, supportive relationships into my life."

– Use present tense: Phrase your affirmations in the present tense, as if they are already true. For example, instead of saying "I will be successful," say "I am successful."

– Keep them positive: Focus on positive statements that affirm your worth and potential. Avoid affirmations that are negative or self-critical.

– Repeat them often: Repeat your affirmations regularly, either out loud or silently. You can also write them down and post them in a place where you will see them frequently.

– Believe in them: Affirmations are most effective when we truly believe in them. If you find yourself struggling to believe your affirmations, take some time to work through any underlying beliefs or self-doubt that may be holding you back.

Incorporating affirmations into your daily routine can help you to cultivate a more positive mindset, build your self-confidence, and achieve your goals. So take some time to create affirmations that resonate with you, and see how they can help transform your life.

08: AFFIRMATIONS AND THEIR POWER

When creating affirmations, it's important to choose statements that are meaningful and relevant to your life. You might choose affirmations that are focused on specific goals, such as career success or improved relationships. Or you might choose affirmations that are focused on general areas of your life, such as self-esteem or inner peace.

Here are some examples of affirmations that you might find helpful:

– I am capable of achieving my goals and dreams.

– I trust in my abilities and my intuition.

– I am confident in myself and my decisions.

– I am worthy of love and respect.

– I am grateful for all of the abundance in my life.

– I choose to focus on the positive and let go of negativity.

– I am at peace with myself and my circumstances.

– I am creating a fulfilling and joyful life for myself.

When using affirmations, it's important to remember that

they are not a magical solution to all of life's problems. Affirmations are a tool to help shift your mindset and beliefs in a more positive direction, but they work best when used in conjunction with other positive practices, such as gratitude, visualization, and self-care.

It's also important to be patient and consistent when using affirmations. Changing your thoughts and beliefs takes time and effort, and it's normal to experience resistance or doubts along the way. But with continued practice and commitment, affirmations can be a powerful tool for creating positive change in your life.

In addition to using affirmations for yourself, you can also use them to support and uplift others. Encouraging friends and loved ones with positive affirmations can help them to feel supported and empowered, and can strengthen your relationships.

In summary, affirmations are a powerful tool for cultivating a more positive mindset, building self-confidence and self-esteem, and achieving your goals. By choosing affirmations that resonate with you, and using them consistently and with intention, you can transform your thoughts and beliefs, and create a more fulfilling and joyful life.

09: Mindfulness Techniques for Positive Thinking

Mindfulness is a practice that involves being fully present and aware in the present moment, without judgment or distraction. When it comes to positive thinking, mindfulness can be a powerful tool for reducing stress and anxiety, increasing self-awareness, and cultivating a more positive mindset. In this chapter, we will explore mindfulness techniques that can help you to harness the power of your mind and transform your life.

– Mindful Breathing: One of the simplest and most effective mindfulness techniques is mindful breathing. To practice this technique, simply take a few deep breaths and focus your attention on the sensation of your breath moving in and out of your body. Notice the rise and fall of your chest, the sensation of the air moving through your nose or mouth, and any other physical sensations that arise. If your mind wanders, gently bring your attention back to your breath.

– Body Scan Meditation: Another mindfulness technique is body scan meditation, which involves paying attention to each part of your body in turn, from your toes to the top of your head. Start by finding a comfortable position, either sitting or lying down, and close your eyes. Take a few deep breaths, and then start to focus your attention on your feet. Notice any sensations you feel in your feet, such as warmth, tingling, or pressure, and then move your attention slowly up your body, noticing any sensations you feel in each part of your body.

– Gratitude Meditation: Gratitude is an important component of positive thinking, and gratitude meditation is a mindfulness technique that can help you to cultivate feelings of gratitude and appreciation. To practice gratitude meditation, start by finding a comfortable position and taking a few deep breaths. Then, bring to mind someone or something that you feel grateful for. Visualize that person or thing in your mind's eye, and think about all of the ways in which they have enriched your life. Allow yourself to feel a sense of gratitude and appreciation for that person or thing.

– Mindful Movement: Mindful movement, such as yoga or tai chi, can be a powerful way to cultivate mindfulness and positive thinking. These practices involve moving your body in a slow, deliberate, and mindful way, while focusing your attention on your breath and the sensations in your body. Not only can these practices help to reduce stress and anxiety, but they can also help to increase flexibility, strength, and balance.

– Mindful Eating: Mindful eating is a practice that involves paying close attention to the experience of eating, without distractions or judgments. To practice mindful eating, choose a food that you enjoy and take a small bite. Chew the food slowly and deliberately, noticing the taste, texture, and sensations in your mouth. Try to savor each bite and be fully present in the experience of eating.

– Mindful Listening: Mindful listening is a technique that can help you to improve your communication skills and deepen your connections with others. To practice mindful listening, choose a person to talk to and give them your full attention. Focus on what they are saying, without interrupting or trying to formulate a response. Notice the tone of their voice, their body language, and any emotions that arise in yourself as you listen. When they are finished speaking, take a moment to reflect on what they said before responding.

09: MINDFULNESS TECHNIQUES FOR POSITIVE THINKING

– Mindful Walking: Mindful walking is a technique that involves walking slowly and deliberately, while focusing your attention on your breath and the sensations in your body. This technique can be practiced indoors or outdoors, and can be a great way to incorporate mindfulness into your daily routine. As you walk, focus on the sensations of your feet touching the ground, the movement of your body, and the rhythm of your breath.

– Loving-Kindness Meditation: Loving-kindness meditation is a mindfulness technique that involves cultivating feelings of love, compassion, and kindness towards yourself and others. To practice this technique, start by finding a comfortable position and taking a few deep breaths. Then, bring to mind someone you love and repeat the following phrases silently to yourself: "May you be happy. May you be healthy. May you be safe. May you live with ease." Repeat these phrases several times, allowing yourself to feel a sense of love and compassion for the person you are visualizing. Then, repeat the phrases for yourself, and for all beings everywhere.

– Mindful Journaling: Journaling can be a powerful tool for

self-reflection and personal growth, and when combined with mindfulness, it can be even more transformative. To practice mindful journaling, set aside a few minutes each day to write down your thoughts and feelings. As you write, focus on the physical sensations of writing, and notice any thoughts or emotions that arise. Write without judgment, and allow yourself to be fully present in the experience of journaling.

– Mindful Pause: Finally, one of the simplest and most effective mindfulness techniques is the mindful pause. Whenever you feel overwhelmed or stressed, take a moment to pause and bring your attention to your breath. Take a few deep breaths, and focus on the sensation of the air moving in and out of your body. This simple practice can help you to feel more centered and grounded, and can be done anytime, anywhere.

By incorporating these mindfulness techniques into your daily routine, you can cultivate a more positive mindset, reduce stress and anxiety, and create a greater sense of overall well-being. Remember, mindfulness is a practice that requires consistency and commitment, so start small and be

patient with yourself. With time and effort, you can transform your thoughts and beliefs, and create a more fulfilling
and joyful life.

10: The Impact of Positive Thinking on Health

The mind and body are interconnected, and research has shown that positive thinking can have a profound impact on our physical health. When we engage in positive thinking, we reduce stress, increase our sense of well-being, and strengthen our immune system. In this chapter, we will explore the ways in which positive thinking can affect our health, and offer tips for incorporating positive thinking into your daily routine.

Reducing Stress: Stress is a common factor in many health problems, from headaches and muscle tension to heart disease and digestive issues. When we experience stress, our bodies release cortisol and other stress hormones, which can have negative effects on our physical and mental health. Positive thinking can help to reduce stress by promoting feelings of relaxation, calmness, and well-being. Studies have shown that people who engage in positive thinking techniques like visualization, gratitude, and meditation experience lower levels of stress hormones and report feeling more relaxed and calm.

Strengthening the Immune System: Our immune system is

responsible for protecting us against illness and disease, and positive thinking can play a role in strengthening our immune response. Research has shown that positive thinking can increase the production of immune cells, reduce inflammation, and improve overall immune function. In addition, people who engage in positive thinking techniques like visualization and meditation have been shown to recover more quickly from illness and injury.

Improving Cardiovascular Health: Positive thinking can have a positive impact on our cardiovascular health as well. Studies have shown that people who engage in positive thinking techniques like gratitude and visualization have lower blood pressure and a reduced risk of heart disease. In addition, positive thinking can help to improve circulation and reduce inflammation, both of which can contribute to better cardiovascular health.

Enhancing Mental Health: Positive thinking can have a profound impact on our mental health as well. People who engage in positive thinking techniques like gratitude, affirmations, and visualization have been shown to experience less anxiety and depression, and report higher levels of life satisfaction and well-being. In addition, positive thinking can help to improve cognitive function, increase resilience, and enhance overall mental clarity and focus.

Incorporating Positive Thinking into Your Daily Routine: If you want to experience the health benefits of positive thinking, there are many techniques you can use to cultivate a more positive mindset. Some simple strategies include practicing gratitude, visualization, affirmations, and mindfulness meditation. You can also make a conscious effort to focus on the positive aspects of your life, and surround yourself with positive people and environments. By incorporating these techniques into your daily routine, you can cultivate a more positive mindset, reduce stress, and enhance your overall health and well-being.

Conclusion: Positive thinking has the power to transform our health and well-being, and it's never too late to start cultivating a more positive mindset. Whether you are dealing with a health challenge or simply want to enhance your overall sense of well-being, incorporating positive thinking techniques into your daily routine can have a profound impact on your physical, mental, and emotional health. Remember to be patient with yourself and consistent in your practice, and trust in the power of positive thinking to help you achieve your health and wellness goals.

Here are some additional tips for incorporating positive thinking into your daily routine:

– Practice gratitude journaling: Every day, write down three things you are grateful for. This can help you focus on the positive aspects of your life and cultivate a more positive mindset.

– Use positive affirmations: Choose a positive statement or affirmation and repeat it to yourself throughout the day. This can help to counteract negative self-talk and promote feelings of self-confidence and self-worth.

– Visualize your goals: Spend a few minutes each day visualizing yourself achieving your goals. This can help to increase motivation and focus, and can also help you to overcome obstacles and setbacks.

– Practice mindfulness meditation: Mindfulness meditation involves focusing your attention on the present moment without judgment. This can help to reduce stress and promote feelings of calmness and relaxation.

– Surround yourself with positivity: Make a conscious effort to spend time with positive people, engage in activities that bring you joy, and create a home and work environment that is uplifting and supportive.

Remember, positive thinking is a skill that can be developed with practice and persistence. By incorporating these techniques into your daily routine, you can cultivate a more positive mindset and enhance your overall health and well-being.

11: Cultivating Positive Relationships

Cultivating positive relationships is an essential aspect of positive thinking and overall well-being. Positive relationships can enhance our sense of belonging, provide emotional support, and promote positive behaviors and attitudes. In contrast, negative relationships can cause stress, conflict, and emotional distress. In this chapter, we will explore some strategies for cultivating positive relationships and enhancing the quality of our social connections.

– Practice active listening: One of the most important aspects of cultivating positive relationships is being a good listener. This involves paying attention to what the other person is saying, asking questions, and showing empathy and understanding. By practicing active listening, you can deepen your connection with others and foster a greater sense of trust and respect.

– Communicate effectively: Effective communication is key to building positive relationships. This involves expressing your thoughts and feelings clearly and respectfully, listening to others, and being open to feedback. By communicating effectively, you can avoid misunderstandings, resolve conflicts, and build stronger, more meaningful relationships.

– Build trust: Trust is a crucial component of positive relationships. Trust is built through consistent actions, honesty, and reliability. By following through on your commitments, being truthful, and showing respect and consideration for others, you can build a foundation of trust and strengthen your relationships.

– Show appreciation: Expressing gratitude and appreciation can help to enhance positive relationships. This involves acknowledging the efforts and contributions of others, and showing gratitude for their support and assistance. By showing appreciation, you can enhance feelings of positivity and mutual respect in your relationships.

– Practice forgiveness: Forgiveness is another key component of positive relationships. Holding onto grudges and resentments can cause tension and conflict in relationships. By practicing forgiveness and letting go of past hurts, you can promote healing and enhance the quality of your relationships.

– Set healthy boundaries: Setting healthy boundaries is essential for maintaining positive relationships. This involves clearly communicating your needs and limits, and respecting the needs and limits of others. By setting healthy boundaries, you can promote mutual respect and reduce the likelihood of conflicts and misunderstandings.

– Practice empathy: Empathy is the ability to understand and share the feelings of others. By practicing empathy, you can deepen your connection with others and promote positive relationships. This involves putting yourself in the other person's shoes, acknowledging their emotions, and showing compassion and understanding.

– Be supportive: Being supportive is an essential aspect of positive relationships. This involves offering help, encouragement, and emotional support to those who need it. By being supportive, you can enhance feelings of positivity and mutual respect in your relationships and foster a sense of trust and connection.

– Practice active participation: Active participation is the act of engaging fully in social situations and being present in the moment. By practicing active participation, you can enhance your connection with others and promote positive relationships. This involves being fully engaged in conversations, actively participating in social activities, and showing a genuine interest in others.

– Be mindful of non-verbal communication: Non-verbal communication can have a significant impact on the quality of our social interactions. By being mindful of your body language, tone of voice, and facial expressions, you can enhance your communication with others and promote positive relationships. This involves being aware of your non-verbal cues and adjusting them as needed to promote positive interactions and enhance your relationships.

In summary, cultivating positive relationships involves a combination of active listening, effective communication, building trust, showing appreciation, practicing forgiveness, setting healthy boundaries, practicing empathy, being supportive, practicing active participation, and being mindful of non-verbal communication. By incorporating these strategies into your daily interactions, you can enhance the quality of your relationships and promote a greater sense of positivity and well-being in your life.

12: Positive Thinking and Personal Growth

Positive thinking can play a powerful role in personal growth. When we think positively, we are more likely to have a growth mindset, which allows us to embrace challenges, persist through setbacks, and ultimately achieve our goals. In this chapter, we will explore the relationship between positive thinking and personal growth and discuss practical strategies for cultivating positivity and achieving personal growth.

– Embrace challenges: Positive thinking allows us to embrace challenges and view them as opportunities for growth. Rather than shying away from challenges or feeling discouraged by setbacks, we can approach them with a growth mindset and see them as chances to learn and develop.

– Learn from failures: Failure is an inevitable part of the growth process, but it can be challenging to overcome. Positive thinking can help us to view failures as learning opportunities and identify the lessons we can take away from them. By focusing on what we can learn from our failures, we can use them as stepping stones to future success.

– Set goals: Setting goals is an important aspect of personal growth, and positive thinking can help us to achieve them. By setting realistic and achievable goals, we can create a clear roadmap for our personal growth and celebrate our progress along the way.

– Believe in yourself: Believing in ourselves is essential to personal growth. When we have a positive outlook and believe in our abilities, we are more likely to take risks, push ourselves out of our comfort zones, and achieve our goals. By cultivating a sense of self-confidence and self-efficacy, we can foster a growth mindset and achieve personal growth.

– Seek feedback: Feedback is an essential part of personal growth, but it can be challenging to receive. Positive thinking can help us to view feedback as a gift and an opportunity for growth, rather than criticism. By seeking out constructive feedback and using it to improve ourselves, we can accelerate our personal growth and achieve our goals more quickly.

– Practice self-reflection: Self-reflection is a valuable tool for personal growth, allowing us to gain insight into our thoughts, feelings, and behaviors. By practicing self-reflection regularly and using it to identify areas for growth, we can develop a deeper understanding of ourselves and cultivate a growth mindset.

– Surround yourself with positivity: Our environment can have a significant impact on our mindset and personal growth. By surrounding ourselves with positive people, inspirational messages, and uplifting experiences, we can enhance our sense of well-being and promote personal growth.

– Challenge limiting beliefs: Our beliefs can be a significant barrier to personal growth, particularly when they are negative or limiting. Positive thinking can help us to challenge these beliefs and develop a more growth-oriented mindset. By identifying and questioning our limiting beliefs, we can create space for new possibilities and opportunities for personal growth.

– Cultivate resilience: Resilience is an essential skill for personal growth, enabling us to bounce back from setbacks and challenges. Positive thinking can help us to cultivate resilience by focusing on our strengths and resources, rather than our weaknesses and limitations. By developing a growth mindset and a sense of self-efficacy, we can build our resilience and persevere through difficult times.

– Practice self-care: Self-care is critical for personal growth, enabling us to nurture our physical, emotional, and mental well-being. Positive thinking can help us to prioritize self-care by promoting a sense of self-compassion and self-love. By taking care of ourselves and practicing self-compassion, we can enhance our personal growth and well-being.

– Learn new skills: Personal growth involves learning and development, and positive thinking can help us to embrace new skills and experiences. By adopting a growth mindset and seeking out new opportunities for learning, we can expand our knowledge and abilities and achieve our goals more effectively.

– Celebrate progress: Celebrating progress is an important aspect of personal growth, allowing us to acknowledge our achievements and build our confidence. Positive thinking can help us to celebrate progress by focusing on our successes and strengths, rather than our failures and limitations. By celebrating our progress and recognizing our accomplishments, we can stay motivated and continue to grow and develop.

In conclusion, positive thinking is a powerful tool for personal growth, enabling us to embrace challenges, learn from failures, set goals, believe in ourselves, seek feedback, practice self-reflection, and surround ourselves with positivity. By cultivating a growth mindset and incorporating these strategies into our daily lives, we can enhance our personal growth and achieve our goals with greater ease and satisfaction. Personal growth is an ongoing process, and positive thinking can help us to navigate the challenges and opportunities that arise along the way.

13: Navigating Setbacks and Challenges with Positivity

Setbacks and challenges are an inevitable part of life, and they can be particularly challenging to navigate when we are trying to maintain a positive outlook. However, with the right mindset and tools, we can use positivity to help us overcome obstacles and emerge stronger on the other side. In this chapter, we will explore some strategies for navigating setbacks and challenges with positivity.

– Acceptance: The first step in navigating setbacks and challenges is to accept the situation for what it is. This does not mean that we have to like or approve of what is happening, but it does mean that we need to acknowledge and accept it. By accepting the situation, we can avoid wasting energy and resources on denial or resistance and focus on finding solutions.

– Positive self-talk: Self-talk is the inner dialogue we have with ourselves, and it can have a significant impact on our mindset and well-being. During setbacks and challenges, it is essential to maintain positive self-talk and avoid negative or self-defeating thoughts. By reframing our thoughts in a positive way, we can maintain a sense of hope and optimism.

– Seek support: Setbacks and challenges can be isolating, and it is important to seek support from friends, family, or a professional if needed. By sharing our struggles with others, we can gain new perspectives, receive encouragement and validation, and feel less alone.

– Practice gratitude: Gratitude is a powerful antidote to negativity, and it can help us to maintain a positive mindset during setbacks and challenges. By focusing on what we are grateful for, we can shift our attention away from the problem and towards the positive aspects of our lives.

– Embrace the learning opportunity: Setbacks and challenges can provide valuable learning opportunities if we approach them with the right mindset. By reframing setbacks as opportunities for growth and learning, we can extract lessons from the experience and emerge stronger and wiser.

– Set realistic goals: During setbacks and challenges, it can be easy to become overwhelmed and lose sight of our goals. It is important to set realistic and achievable goals to maintain a sense of momentum and progress. By breaking larger goals into smaller, manageable steps, we can avoid feeling overwhelmed and stay motivated.

– Practice self-care: Self-care is essential during setbacks and challenges, as it can help us to maintain our physical, emotional, and mental well-being. By taking care of ourselves and prioritizing self-care activities such as exercise, meditation, or a hobby, we can recharge and re-energize ourselves to face the challenges ahead.

– Embrace positivity: Finally, it is important to embrace positivity as a guiding principle during setbacks and challenges. By cultivating a positive mindset and focusing on the opportunities and possibilities that exist within the challenge, we can remain optimistic and resilient.

In conclusion, setbacks and challenges can be difficult to navigate, but with the right mindset and tools, we can use positivity to overcome them. By accepting the situation, practicing positive self-talk, seeking support, practicing gratitude, embracing the learning opportunity, setting realistic goals, practicing self-care, and embracing positivity, we can emerge stronger and more resilient on the other side. Remember, setbacks and challenges are a part of life, but with positivity, we can face them head-on and emerge victorious.

In order to navigate setbacks and challenges with positivity, it's important to have the right mindset and tools in place. Here are some strategies for maintaining a positive attitude in the face of adversity:

– Reframe negative thoughts: When faced with a setback or challenge, it's easy to slip into negative self-talk or catastrophizing. Instead, try to reframe the situation in a more positive light. Ask yourself what you can learn from the experience, or what opportunities might arise as a result of it.

– Focus on solutions: Rather than dwelling on the problem, focus your energy on finding solutions. Brainstorm a list of potential solutions, and then take action on the most promising ones. Remember that even small steps forward can make a big difference in the long run.

– Practice self-compassion: It's natural to feel frustrated or disappointed when things don't go as planned. But instead of beating yourself up, practice self-compassion. Remind yourself that setbacks are a normal part of life, and that you are doing your best. Treat yourself with kindness and understanding.

– Stay connected: When faced with a challenge, it's easy to isolate yourself or withdraw from social connections. But staying connected to others can be a powerful source of support and positivity. Reach out to friends, family, or a support group for encouragement and advice.

– Stay in the present moment: It's easy to get caught up in worries about the future or regrets about the past. But staying in the present moment can help you stay grounded and focused. Practice mindfulness techniques such as deep breathing, meditation, or yoga to help you stay centered.

– Practice gratitude: When things are tough, it can be easy to focus on what's going wrong. But taking time to reflect on what you're grateful for can help shift your perspective and boost your mood. Make a list of things you're grateful for each day, no matter how small.

By incorporating these strategies into your life, you can develop a more positive mindset and navigate setbacks and challenges with greater resilience and grace. Remember, positivity is a muscle that can be strengthened with practice and intention.

14: The Benefits of a Positive Work Environment

A positive work environment is one in which employees feel valued, supported, and empowered. There are many benefits to creating such an environment, including:

– Increased productivity: When employees feel good about their work environment, they are more likely to be motivated and engaged. This can lead to increased productivity and better overall performance.

– Improved morale: A positive work environment can boost morale and create a sense of camaraderie among employees. This can lead to a more positive and supportive workplace culture, which can in turn improve retention rates and reduce turnover.

– Better communication: When employees feel comfortable and supported, they are more likely to communicate openly and honestly with one another. This can lead to better collaboration, more effective problem-solving, and a stronger sense of teamwork.

– Increased creativity: A positive work environment can

foster creativity and innovation by encouraging employees to take risks and think outside the box. This can lead to new ideas and approaches, which can in turn help the organization stay competitive and relevant.

– Better employee health: A positive work environment can also have a positive impact on employee health. When employees feel stressed or unhappy at work, it can take a toll on their physical and mental health. By creating a more positive and supportive environment, employers can help reduce stress and improve overall well-being.

– Improved customer service: When employees feel supported and valued, they are more likely to provide excellent customer service. This can lead to increased customer satisfaction and loyalty, which can in turn help the organization grow and thrive.

To create a positive work environment, employers can take a number of steps, such as:

– Providing opportunities for professional development and growth

14: THE BENEFITS OF A POSITIVE WORK ENVIRON-
MENT

– Encouraging open communication and feedback

– Recognizing and rewarding employees for their contributions

– Encouraging a healthy work-life balance

– Promoting a culture of inclusion and diversity

– Providing a safe and comfortable work environment

– Encouraging teamwork and collaboration

By investing in a positive work environment, employers can reap the benefits of a more engaged, productive, and loyal workforce.

Creating a positive work environment takes time and effort, but the benefits are well worth it. Here are some additional strategies that employers can use to cultivate a positive workplace:

– Lead by example: Employers and managers should model positive behaviors and attitudes, such as active listening, empathy, and constructive feedback. When employees see their leaders embodying these qualities, they are more likely to follow suit.

– Encourage social connections: Encourage employees to build relationships with one another by organizing social events or team-building activities. This can help create a sense of community and belonging within the workplace.

– Provide opportunities for feedback: Employees should be given regular opportunities to share their thoughts and ideas with their supervisors and colleagues. This can help ensure that everyone feels heard and valued.

– Celebrate achievements: When employees achieve milestones or reach important goals, be sure to recognize and celebrate their accomplishments. This can help build morale and reinforce a culture of positivity.

– Be flexible: Employers should strive to be flexible and accommodating when possible, such as by offering flexible work hours or remote work options. This can help employees feel valued and supported, which can in turn lead to greater job satisfaction.

14: THE BENEFITS OF A POSITIVE WORK ENVIRONMENT

– Foster a learning culture: Encourage employees to learn and grow by offering opportunities for training and development. This can help employees feel more engaged and invested in their work, while also improving their skills and knowledge.

– Focus on the positive: Finally, employers should strive to create a culture that focuses on the positive. Instead of dwelling on mistakes or problems, emphasize the positive aspects of the workplace and encourage employees to do the same.

By implementing these strategies, employers can create a workplace that is supportive, engaging, and positive. This can lead to a more productive, motivated, and satisfied workforce, which can in turn help the organization achieve its goals and succeed in a competitive marketplace.

15: Positive Parenting and Child Development

Positive parenting is a parenting approach that emphasizes the use of positive reinforcement, open communication, and empathy to build strong, healthy relationships with children. Positive parenting has been shown to have numerous benefits for both children and parents, including improved behavior, greater self-esteem, and stronger bonds.

Here are some key principles of positive parenting:

– Use positive reinforcement: Instead of punishing negative behavior, focus on rewarding positive behavior. This can include verbal praise, physical affection, or small rewards like stickers or tokens.

– Be consistent: Consistency is key when it comes to positive parenting. Be clear and consistent with rules and expectations, and follow through with consequences when necessary.

– Use open communication: Encourage open communication with your child by actively listening and showing empathy. Try to understand their perspective and validate their feelings.

– Set boundaries: It's important to set clear boundaries and rules for your child, but do so in a positive and constructive way. Explain the reasons behind the rules and encourage your child to participate in problem-solving when conflicts arise.

– Focus on the relationship: Above all, positive parenting is about building strong, healthy relationships with your children. Focus on building trust, respect, and open communication.

Positive parenting has been shown to have numerous benefits for child development. Studies have found that children who experience positive parenting have better mental health outcomes, including lower rates of anxiety and depression. Positive parenting has also been linked to improved behavior, including lower rates of aggression and delinquency.

In addition to these benefits for children, positive parenting can also have benefits for parents. By emphasizing positive reinforcement and open communication, parents can reduce stress and improve their own mental health. Positive parenting can also help parents build stronger relationships with their children, which can lead to greater satisfaction and fulfillment in parenting.

To practice positive parenting, try to be patient, consistent, and empathetic with your child. Focus on building a strong, healthy relationship based on trust and open communication. Remember that positive reinforcement is more effective than punishment, and that setting clear boundaries and expectations can help your child feel safe and secure.

By adopting a positive parenting approach, you can help your child thrive and develop into a happy, healthy, and well-adjusted adult.

When it comes to child development, positive parenting can also foster important life skills and character traits. For example, children who experience positive parenting are more likely to develop strong social skills, including empathy, communication, and problem-solving. They may also develop a greater sense of autonomy and independence, as positive parenting encourages children to take responsibility for their own behavior and decisions.

Positive parenting can also promote a growth mindset in

children, which is the belief that abilities and intelligence can be developed through hard work and dedication. By focusing on effort and progress rather than innate ability, positive parenting can help children develop a sense of resilience and persistence in the face of challenges.

Another important aspect of positive parenting is modeling positive behavior. Children learn by example, and parents who model positive attitudes and behaviors are more likely to have children who adopt those same attitudes and behaviors. This includes things like practicing gratitude, using positive self-talk, and treating others with kindness and respect.

Overall, positive parenting is a powerful tool for promoting child development and building strong, healthy relationships with children. By focusing on positive reinforcement, open communication, and empathy, parents can help their children thrive and develop into happy, healthy, and well-adjusted adults.

16: Overcoming Fear and Anxiety with Positive Thinking

Fear and anxiety are natural emotions that everyone experiences from time to time. However, when these feelings become overwhelming and interfere with daily life, they can be difficult to manage. Fortunately, positive thinking can be an effective tool for overcoming fear and anxiety and regaining control of one's life.

One of the key ways that positive thinking can help overcome fear and anxiety is by reframing negative thoughts into positive ones. When faced with a fearful or anxiety-provoking situation, it's common for people to have negative thoughts and beliefs, such as "I can't handle this" or "Something bad is going to happen." These thoughts can fuel feelings of fear and anxiety, making it difficult to move forward.

Positive thinking involves challenging these negative thoughts and replacing them with more positive, realistic ones. For example, "I have faced difficult situations before and have overcome them" or "I have the tools and resources to handle this situation." By focusing on positive thoughts and beliefs, people can shift their mindset from one of fear and anxiety to one of confidence and optimism.

16: OVERCOMING FEAR AND ANXIETY WITH POSITIVE THINKING

Another way that positive thinking can help overcome fear and anxiety is by using relaxation and mindfulness techniques. These can include deep breathing exercises, meditation, or visualization. These techniques can help people relax and reduce physical symptoms of anxiety, such as rapid heartbeat or shortness of breath.

Positive thinking can also involve focusing on one's strengths and successes. By reflecting on past accomplishments and recognizing personal strengths, people can boost their confidence and feel more capable of handling challenges.

Finally, positive thinking can involve seeking support from others. Talking to a trusted friend or therapist can provide a safe space to express fears and anxieties and receive guidance and support.

Overall, positive thinking can be a powerful tool for overcoming fear and anxiety. By reframing negative thoughts, using relaxation techniques, focusing on strengths, and seeking support, people can overcome their fears and live more fulfilling lives.

16: OVERCOMING FEAR AND ANXIETY WITH POSITIVE THINKING

In addition to these strategies, there are several other ways that positive thinking can help overcome fear and anxiety. These include:

– Emphasizing the present moment: Fear and anxiety often stem from worries about the future or regrets about the past. By focusing on the present moment and engaging in mindfulness practices, individuals can reduce feelings of fear and anxiety.

– Practicing self-care: Taking care of one's physical and emotional needs is crucial for managing anxiety and reducing stress. This can include regular exercise, healthy eating habits, and getting enough sleep.

– Setting achievable goals: Setting goals and working towards them can provide a sense of purpose and direction, reducing feelings of anxiety and uncertainty.

– Cultivating a positive support system: Surrounding oneself with positive and supportive people can provide a sense of comfort and security, reducing feelings of anxiety.

– Practicing gratitude: Focusing on the positive aspects of

one's life and expressing gratitude for them can shift one's mindset from one of anxiety to one of positivity and appreciation.

It's important to note that positive thinking is not a quick fix for overcoming fear and anxiety. It takes time and effort to develop a positive mindset and learn to manage anxious thoughts and feelings. However, by incorporating positive thinking strategies into one's daily life and seeking support from others, it is possible to overcome fear and anxiety and live a more fulfilling life.

17: Overcoming Procrastination and Boosting Productivity

Procrastination is a common issue that can lead to decreased productivity, missed deadlines, and increased stress levels. However, by incorporating positive thinking techniques, individuals can overcome procrastination and boost their productivity. Here are some strategies for overcoming procrastination:

– Setting clear goals and deadlines: Setting specific, achievable goals and deadlines can help individuals stay motivated and focused on their tasks.

– Breaking tasks into smaller, manageable steps: Large tasks can be overwhelming and lead to procrastination. By breaking tasks into smaller steps, individuals can make progress without feeling overwhelmed.

– Using positive self-talk: Positive self-talk can help individuals overcome negative thoughts and beliefs that can lead to procrastination. Encouraging and motivating self-talk can increase confidence and reduce feelings of overwhelm.

– Taking breaks and practicing self-care: Taking regular breaks and practicing self-care activities can help individuals recharge and reduce stress levels. This can increase motivation and reduce the urge to procrastinate.

– Practicing visualization: Visualizing the end result of completing a task can increase motivation and reduce procrastination. By imagining how good it will feel to have completed the task, individuals can overcome the initial resistance to starting.

– Surrounding oneself with positive influences: Being around positive and motivated individuals can be contagious. By surrounding oneself with positive influences, individuals can increase their own motivation and productivity levels.

In addition to these strategies, individuals can also benefit from developing a positive mindset and cultivating a sense of gratitude. Focusing on the positive aspects of one's life can increase motivation and reduce procrastination. Additionally, celebrating small accomplishments along the way can increase motivation and reduce the urge to procrastinate.

17: OVERCOMING PROCRASTINATION AND BOOSTING PRODUCTIVITY

Overall, overcoming procrastination requires a combination of strategies and a commitment to developing a positive mindset. By incorporating positive thinking techniques and focusing on achievable goals, individuals can overcome procrastination and boost their productivity.

It is important to note that boosting productivity is not just about getting things done quickly, but also about doing things well. Therefore, it is important to prioritize tasks and focus on those that are most important and will have the biggest impact. This can help individuals stay motivated and avoid getting bogged down by less important tasks.

Additionally, it is important to practice self-compassion and not be too hard on oneself when setbacks or delays occur. Negative self-talk and self-criticism can lead to feelings of overwhelm and decrease motivation. Instead, individuals should focus on their strengths and accomplishments, and use positive self-talk to motivate themselves.

Another key aspect of boosting productivity is taking care of one's physical health. Eating a balanced diet, getting enough sleep, and engaging in regular exercise can increase energy levels and reduce stress, which can have a positive impact on productivity. Taking breaks throughout the day, even if just for a few minutes, can also help individuals recharge and stay focused.

Finally, it is important to remember that boosting productivity is a continuous process that requires ongoing effort and dedication. It may take time to develop positive thinking habits and overcome procrastination, but with patience and persistence, it is possible to achieve greater productivity and success in all areas of life.

18: The Role of Positive Thinking in Goal Setting

The power of positive thinking can have a significant impact on setting and achieving goals. Positive thinking can help individuals develop a growth mindset, increase motivation, and overcome obstacles that may prevent them from reaching their goals.

To begin, it is important to have a clear vision of what one wants to achieve. Setting specific, measurable, achievable, relevant, and time-bound (SMART) goals can help individuals focus their efforts and stay on track. Having a positive attitude towards these goals can further enhance motivation and persistence.

One of the key aspects of positive thinking in goal setting is focusing on what is within one's control. While there may be external factors that can impact the outcome of a goal, individuals should focus on the aspects of the goal that they can control. This can include developing a plan of action, identifying resources and support, and taking steps towards achieving the goal.

Another important aspect of positive thinking in goal set-

ting is overcoming limiting beliefs. Limiting beliefs are negative thoughts or beliefs that can prevent individuals from
achieving their goals. These can include beliefs such as "I'm
not good enough" or "I don't have enough time". By identifying and challenging these beliefs, individuals can develop
a more positive mindset and increase their chances of success.

Positive thinking can also help individuals overcome
obstacles and setbacks that may occur during the goal-set-
ting process. Instead of giving up when faced with a setback,
individuals can use positive thinking to reframe the situation and focus on the opportunities for growth and learning that may arise from the setback.

Additionally, positive thinking can help individuals stay focused on their goals and maintain motivation over the long
term. By focusing on the positive aspects of the goal and the
progress that has been made, individuals can stay committed to their goals and persevere through challenges.

In conclusion, positive thinking plays a critical role in setting and achieving goals. By maintaining a positive attitude,
focusing on what is within one's control, overcoming limit-

ing beliefs, and staying motivated through setbacks and obstacles, individuals can increase their chances of success and achieve their desired outcomes.

Once you have a positive mindset and have overcome negative thoughts, you can begin to focus on setting goals for yourself. Positive thinking can play a critical role in goal setting because it allows you to visualize and work towards a positive outcome. When you have a positive attitude and believe in yourself, you are more likely to set ambitious goals and work hard to achieve them.

Here are some ways in which positive thinking can help you set and achieve your goals:

– Increases motivation: When you think positively, you feel more motivated to work towards your goals. You believe in yourself and your ability to succeed, which makes it easier to stay focused and dedicated.

– Helps you overcome obstacles: When you encounter obstacles or setbacks, a positive attitude can help you overcome them more easily. Instead of giving up or getting discouraged, you can look at the situation as a learning opportunity and use it to grow and improve.

– Keeps you focused on the end result: With a positive mindset, you can keep your eyes on the prize and stay motivated to achieve your goals. You are less likely to get sidetracked or distracted by minor setbacks or obstacles.

– Increases creativity and problem-solving abilities: When you are positive, you are more likely to think creatively and come up with innovative solutions to problems. This can be incredibly helpful when working towards a goal, as it allows you to approach challenges in new and exciting ways.

– Improves your self-esteem: When you have a positive attitude, you feel better about yourself and your abilities. This increased self-esteem can help you set more ambitious goals and believe in yourself even when things get tough.

To make the most of positive thinking in goal setting, it's important to be clear about what you want to achieve and why. Set specific, measurable goals that are challenging but achievable. Break down your goals into smaller, more manageable steps and focus on one step at a time.

19: Positive Thinking and Financial Success

Positive thinking is a powerful tool that can help you achieve financial success. The way you think about money and your ability to attract wealth can have a significant impact on your financial situation. In this chapter, we will explore the relationship between positive thinking and financial success and discuss some practical tips to help you adopt a positive mindset.

The power of positive thinking

Positive thinking is the practice of focusing on the positive aspects of a situation and looking for opportunities rather than dwelling on problems or setbacks. Positive thinking can help you overcome obstacles, stay motivated, and achieve your goals.

In the context of finances, positive thinking can help you attract wealth and abundance. By focusing on your financial goals and visualizing yourself achieving them, you can create a positive mindset that will help you take action towards your goals.

19: POSITIVE THINKING AND FINANCIAL SUCCESS

Here are some benefits of positive thinking in relation to financial success:

– Increased motivation: Positive thinking can help you stay motivated and focused on your financial goals, even when faced with challenges or setbacks. When you believe that you can achieve your goals, you are more likely to take action towards them.

– Improved confidence: Positive thinking can boost your confidence and self-esteem, which can help you make better financial decisions and take calculated risks. When you believe in yourself and your ability to succeed, you are more likely to take on challenges and overcome obstacles.

– Better relationships: Positive thinking can also improve your relationships with money and with others. When you have a positive attitude towards money, you are more likely to attract positive financial opportunities and build strong relationships with people who can help you achieve your goals.

Tips for adopting a positive mindset

Here are some practical tips to help you adopt a positive

mindset and attract financial success:

– Set clear financial goals: To create a positive mindset, it is important to have clear financial goals that you are working towards. Write down your goals and visualize yourself achieving them. This will help you stay motivated and focused on your financial goals.

– Focus on abundance: Instead of focusing on what you don't have, focus on abundance and the opportunities that are available to you. When you believe that there is enough wealth and abundance to go around, you are more likely to attract financial success.

– Practice gratitude: Gratitude is a powerful tool for creating a positive mindset. Take time each day to focus on the things that you are grateful for, including your financial blessings. This will help you stay positive and attract more abundance into your life.

– Surround yourself with positivity: Surround yourself with people who have a positive attitude towards money and success. This will help you stay motivated and inspired to achieve your financial goals.

– Stay focused on the present: Instead of worrying about the future or dwelling on the past, focus on the present moment. Take action towards your financial goals and stay focused on the steps you need to take to achieve them.

Positive thinking is a powerful tool for achieving financial success. By adopting a positive mindset and focusing on abundance, you can attract wealth and create a fulfilling financial life. Remember to set clear financial goals, practice gratitude, surround yourself with positivity, and stay focused on the present moment. With these tips, you can achieve financial success and create a life of abundance and prosperity.

It is important to note that positive thinking alone is not enough to achieve financial success. You also need to take action towards your goals and make smart financial decisions. However, a positive mindset can help you overcome obstacles and stay motivated on your financial journey.

Here are some additional tips to help you take action towards your financial goals:

– Create a budget: A budget is a powerful tool for managing your finances and achieving your goals. Create a budget that aligns with your financial goals and stick to it.

– Invest in yourself: Invest in your education and personal development to increase your earning potential and build wealth. Take courses, attend seminars, and read books on personal finance and investing.

– Seek advice from experts: Seek advice from financial experts, such as financial advisors, accountants, and lawyers, to help you make smart financial decisions.

– Avoid debt: Avoid taking on debt that you cannot afford to pay back. Pay off any outstanding debt as soon as possible to free up your financial resources.

– Take calculated risks: Taking calculated risks, such as starting a business or investing in the stock market, can help you build wealth. However, make sure you do your research and seek expert advice before taking any risks.

In summary, positive thinking and financial success are closely related. By adopting a positive mindset and taking action towards your financial goals, you can attract wealth and create a fulfilling financial life. Remember to set clear financial goals, focus on abundance, practice gratitude, surround yourself with positivity, and take action towards your goals. With these tips, you can achieve financial success and create a life of abundance and prosperity.

20: Overcoming Imposter Syndrome with Positive Thinking

Imposter syndrome is a common psychological phenomenon where individuals doubt their accomplishments and fear being exposed as a fraud. It can lead to negative self-talk and self-doubt, which can hinder personal and professional growth. Overcoming imposter syndrome requires a shift in mindset towards positive thinking. In this chapter, we will explore the relationship between positive thinking and imposter syndrome and discuss practical tips to help you overcome imposter syndrome with positive thinking.

The power of positive thinking in overcoming imposter syndrome

Positive thinking is a powerful tool that can help you overcome imposter syndrome. By focusing on your strengths and accomplishments, you can build self-confidence and overcome negative self-talk. Positive thinking can also help you reframe negative thoughts and see challenges as opportunities for growth.

Here are some benefits of positive thinking in relation to overcoming imposter syndrome:

20: OVERCOMING IMPOSTER SYNDROME WITH POSITIVE THINKING

– Improved self-confidence: Positive thinking can help you build self-confidence and trust in your abilities. When you focus on your strengths and accomplishments, you can see yourself as capable and competent, which can help you overcome imposter syndrome.

– Increased resilience: Positive thinking can also help you bounce back from setbacks and challenges. When you see challenges as opportunities for growth and learning, you are more likely to persevere through difficult times.

– Better mental health: Positive thinking can improve your overall mental health and well-being. By focusing on positive thoughts and emotions, you can reduce stress and anxiety, which can contribute to imposter syndrome.

Tips for overcoming imposter syndrome with positive thinking

Here are some practical tips to help you overcome imposter syndrome with positive thinking:

– Acknowledge your accomplishments: Take time to reflect on your accomplishments and the skills that have helped you achieve them. Write them down and refer to them when you are feeling self-doubt.

– Reframe negative thoughts: When negative thoughts arise, reframe them into positive affirmations. For example, if you think "I don't belong here," reframe it as "I bring value to this team and deserve to be here."

– Practice gratitude: Take time each day to focus on the things that you are grateful for, including your accomplishments and the people who support you. This can help you maintain a positive mindset and overcome imposter syndrome.

– Embrace challenges: Instead of fearing challenges, embrace them as opportunities for growth and learning. This can help you develop a growth mindset and build resilience.

– Seek support: Seek support from friends, family, or a therapist. Talking to someone about your feelings can help you gain perspective and overcome imposter syndrome.

Imposter syndrome can be a significant barrier to personal and professional growth. However, by adopting a positive mindset, you can overcome negative self-talk and build self-confidence. Remember to acknowledge your accomplishments, reframe negative thoughts, practice gratitude, embrace challenges, and seek support. With these tips, you can overcome imposter syndrome and achieve your personal and professional goals.

Additionally, it's important to recognize that imposter syndrome can affect anyone, regardless of their background, education, or accomplishments. It is a common experience that affects many people, especially those who are high achievers or who are in positions of leadership.

One way to overcome imposter syndrome is to recognize that it is a normal and common experience. This can help you see that you are not alone in your feelings and that others have overcome similar challenges. By realizing that imposter syndrome is a common experience, you can reduce the power it has over you and gain a sense of perspective.

Another way to overcome imposter syndrome is to focus on your values and purpose. When you focus on your values and purpose, you can see how your work aligns with your personal mission and goals. This can help you feel more connected to your work and confident in your abilities.

Finally, it's important to practice self-compassion. This means treating yourself with kindness and understanding, especially when you make mistakes or experience setbacks. By practicing self-compassion, you can reduce negative self-talk and build a more positive mindset.

In conclusion, overcoming imposter syndrome with positive thinking requires a shift in mindset towards self-compassion, gratitude, and a growth mindset. By focusing on your strengths, accomplishments, and values, you can build self-confidence and resilience, and overcome imposter syndrome. Remember that imposter syndrome is a common experience and that you are not alone in your feelings. With these tips, you can achieve your personal and professional goals and live a more fulfilling life.

21: Building Resilience with Positive Thinking

Resilience is the ability to bounce back from adversity and overcome challenges. It is a valuable trait that can help you cope with stress, overcome obstacles, and achieve your goals. Building resilience requires a positive mindset and the ability to see challenges as opportunities for growth. In this chapter, we will explore the relationship between positive thinking and resilience and discuss practical tips to help you build resilience with positive thinking.

The power of positive thinking in building resilience

Positive thinking is a powerful tool that can help you build resilience. By focusing on positive thoughts and emotions, you can reduce stress and anxiety and increase your ability to cope with adversity. Positive thinking can also help you see challenges as opportunities for growth and change.

Here are some benefits of positive thinking in relation to building resilience:

– Improved mental health: Positive thinking can improve your overall mental health and well-being. By focusing on positive thoughts and emotions, you can reduce stress and anxiety, which can contribute to resilience.

– Increased self-confidence: Positive thinking can help you build self-confidence and trust in your abilities. When you focus on your strengths and accomplishments, you can see yourself as capable and competent, which can help you overcome challenges.

– Better problem-solving skills: Positive thinking can also help you develop better problem-solving skills. When you see challenges as opportunities for growth, you are more likely to approach them with a positive mindset and find creative solutions.

Tips for building resilience with positive thinking

Here are some practical tips to help you build resilience with positive thinking:

– Focus on your strengths: Take time to reflect on your strengths and the skills that have helped you overcome challenges in the past. Write them down and refer to them when you are facing new challenges.

– Practice gratitude: Take time each day to focus on the things that you are grateful for, including the people and experiences that have helped you build resilience. This can help you maintain a positive mindset and build resilience.

– Reframe negative thoughts: When negative thoughts arise, reframe them into positive affirmations. For example, if you think "I can't do this," reframe it as "I have overcome challenges in the past and can do it again."

– Embrace challenges: Instead of fearing challenges, embrace them as opportunities for growth and learning. This can help you develop a growth mindset and build resilience.

– Seek support: Seek support from friends, family, or a therapist. Talking to someone about your challenges can help you gain perspective and build resilience.

– Practice self-care: Self-care is essential for building resilience. Taking care of your physical and mental health can help you cope with stress and adversity. This includes getting enough sleep, eating a healthy diet, exercising regularly, and taking time for relaxation and self-reflection.

– Learn from failure: Failure is a natural part of life and can provide valuable lessons and opportunities for growth. Instead of seeing failure as a setback, learn from it and use it as a stepping stone towards success.

– Set realistic goals: Setting realistic goals can help you build confidence and resilience. Break down larger goals into smaller, achievable steps and celebrate each milestone along the way.

– Practice mindfulness: Mindfulness can help you stay present in the moment and reduce stress and anxiety. Practicing mindfulness techniques, such as deep breathing and meditation, can help you build resilience and improve your overall well-being.

– Stay optimistic: Optimism is an important factor in building resilience. By focusing on positive outcomes and possibilities, you can maintain a positive mindset and build resilience.

Building resilience with positive thinking requires a shift in mindset towards self-compassion, gratitude, and a growth mindset. By focusing on your strengths, accomplishments, and values, you can build self-confidence and resilience, and overcome challenges. Remember to practice gratitude, reframe negative thoughts, embrace challenges, and seek support. With these tips, you can build resilience and achieve your personal and professional goals.

In conclusion, building resilience with positive thinking requires a commitment to self-care, optimism, and a growth mindset. By focusing on your strengths, practicing gratitude, embracing challenges, and seeking support, you can build resilience and overcome adversity. Remember to learn from failure, set realistic goals, practice mindfulness, and stay optimistic. With these tips, you can develop the resilience needed to achieve your personal and professional goals and lead a fulfilling life.

22: The Power of Forgiveness in Positive Thinking

Forgiveness is a powerful tool that can help us move forward in life and achieve greater levels of happiness and fulfillment. Forgiveness is the act of letting go of anger, resentment, and bitterness towards those who have wronged us, and choosing to move forward with compassion and understanding. In this chapter, we will explore the power of forgiveness in positive thinking and discuss practical tips for cultivating forgiveness in our lives.

The benefits of forgiveness in positive thinking

Forgiveness is a powerful tool that can have significant positive effects on our mental and emotional well-being. Here are some benefits of forgiveness in positive thinking:

– Reducing negative emotions: Holding onto anger, resentment, and bitterness can lead to negative emotions, such as anxiety, depression, and stress. Forgiveness can help us let go of these negative emotions and move forward with greater peace and clarity.

– Improving relationships: Forgiveness can help us repair

damaged relationships and build stronger connections with others. By letting go of negative emotions towards others, we can cultivate greater empathy and understanding in our relationships.

– Boosting self-esteem: Forgiveness can also help us boost our self-esteem and confidence. By letting go of negative emotions towards ourselves, we can cultivate greater self-compassion and self-love, which can lead to greater happiness and fulfillment.

– Increasing resilience: Forgiveness can also help us increase our resilience in the face of challenges and adversity. By cultivating forgiveness, we can develop a greater sense of inner strength and resilience, which can help us navigate difficult situations more effectively.

Practical tips for cultivating forgiveness

Here are some practical tips for cultivating forgiveness in our lives:

– Practice empathy: One of the key components of forgiveness is empathy. Practicing empathy involves putting ourselves in the shoes of others and trying to understand their perspective. By cultivating empathy, we can develop greater compassion and forgiveness towards others.

– Let go of anger and resentment: Holding onto anger and resentment only serves to harm ourselves. Letting go of these negative emotions can be a powerful act of self-care and can help us move forward with greater peace and clarity.

– Focus on the present moment: Forgiveness requires us to let go of the past and focus on the present moment. By cultivating mindfulness and staying present, we can let go of past hurts and move forward with greater ease and grace.

– Practice self-compassion: Forgiveness also involves letting go of negative emotions towards ourselves. Practicing self-compassion involves treating ourselves with kindness and understanding, even when we make mistakes or fall short of our expectations.

– Seek support: Forgiveness can be a difficult process, and it is important to seek support from friends, family, or a therapist. Talking through our feelings and experiences with someone we trust can help us gain perspective and cultivate forgiveness.

Forgiveness is a powerful tool that can help us cultivate greater peace, happiness, and fulfillment in our lives. By letting go of anger, resentment, and bitterness towards others and ourselves, we can cultivate greater empathy, compassion, and understanding. Remember to practice empathy, let go of negative emotions, focus on the present moment, practice self-compassion, and seek support. With these tips, we can cultivate forgiveness and experience greater levels of joy and fulfillment in our lives.

Forgiveness can be challenging, especially when we have experienced deep hurt or betrayal. However, the power of forgiveness lies in the fact that it allows us to let go of negative emotions and move forward with greater peace and clarity. It is a journey that requires patience, compassion, and a willingness to let go of past hurts.

Moreover, forgiveness is not the same as forgetting or excusing the actions of others. It is not about pretending that what happened didn't hurt or didn't matter. Forgiveness is about acknowledging the pain and hurt that we experienced, and choosing to let go of the negative emotions that are holding us back. It is a process of healing and growth that allows us to move forward in life with greater peace and happiness.

In conclusion, forgiveness is a powerful tool that can have a significant positive impact on our mental and emotional well-being. By letting go of anger, resentment, and bitterness towards others and ourselves, we can cultivate greater empathy, compassion, and understanding. Remember to practice empathy, let go of negative emotions, focus on the present moment, practice self-compassion, and seek support. With these tips, we can cultivate forgiveness and experience greater levels of joy and fulfillment in our lives.

23: Overcoming Limiting Beliefs and Self-Sabotage

Limiting beliefs and self-sabotage can hold us back from achieving our goals and realizing our full potential. These negative patterns can manifest in various areas of our lives, such as career, relationships, and personal development. In this chapter, we will explore the ways in which limiting beliefs and self-sabotage can affect us, and discuss practical tips for overcoming these patterns and cultivating a positive mindset.

The impact of limiting beliefs and self-sabotage

Limiting beliefs are beliefs that hold us back from achieving our goals and realizing our full potential. These beliefs can be rooted in past experiences, societal expectations, or self-doubt. Some common examples of limiting beliefs include:

– "I'm not good enough"

– "I don't have what it takes to succeed"

– "I don't deserve success and happiness"

– "I'll never be able to achieve my goals"

23: OVERCOMING LIMITING BELIEFS AND SELF-SAB-OTAGE

Self-sabotage, on the other hand, refers to the actions we take that prevent us from achieving our goals or realizing our full potential. These actions can take many forms, such as procrastination, self-doubt, or self-sabotaging behaviors.

Limiting beliefs and self-sabotage can have a significant impact on our lives, leading to feelings of frustration, self-doubt, and unfulfillment. They can hold us back from taking risks, pursuing our passions, and achieving our goals. Overcoming these patterns is essential for cultivating a positive mindset and achieving greater levels of success and happiness.

Tips for overcoming limiting beliefs and self-sabotage

– Identify your limiting beliefs: The first step in overcoming limiting beliefs is to identify them. Take some time to reflect on the negative self-talk and beliefs that hold you back from achieving your goals. Write them down and examine them objectively. Ask yourself if these beliefs are based on fact or if they are just assumptions you've made about yourself.

– Challenge your limiting beliefs: Once you've identified your limiting beliefs, it's time to challenge them. Ask yourself if there is any evidence to support these beliefs. Are they true, or are they just assumptions you've made about yourself? Look for evidence that contradicts your limiting beliefs and use this evidence to challenge and reframe them.

– Practice self-compassion: Overcoming limiting beliefs and self-sabotage can be a challenging process. It's important to practice self-compassion and treat yourself with kindness and understanding. Remember that everyone has limiting beliefs and experiences self-sabotage at times. Don't be too hard on yourself.

– Set realistic goals: Setting realistic goals is an important step in overcoming self-sabotage. When we set goals that are too ambitious or unrealistic, we set ourselves up for failure. Start with small, achievable goals and build up from there.

– Take action: Taking action is essential for overcoming self-sabotage. Procrastination and self-doubt can hold us back from taking action towards our goals. Start with small steps and build momentum over time.

– Surround yourself with positivity: Surrounding yourself

with positivity can help you overcome limiting beliefs and self-sabotage. Spend time with people who support and encourage you. Read books and listen to podcasts that inspire and motivate you.

– Seek support: Overcoming limiting beliefs and self-sabotage can be a challenging process. It's important to seek support from friends, family, or a therapist. Talking through your feelings and experiences with someone you trust can help you gain perspective and cultivate a positive mindset.

Limiting beliefs and self-sabotage can hold us back from achieving our goals and realizing our full potential. Overcoming these patterns is essential for cultivating a positive mindset and achieving greater levels of success and happiness. By identifying our limiting beliefs, challenging them, practicing self-compassion, setting realistic goals, taking action, surrounding ourselves with positivity, and seeking support, we can overcome these negative patterns and cultivate a positive mindset.

Remember that the journey towards overcoming limiting beliefs and self-sabotage is not always easy. It takes time, patience, and consistent effort. However, the rewards of cultivating a positive mindset and achieving our goals are well worth the effort.

When we let go of limiting beliefs and self-sabotage, we open ourselves up to new opportunities and experiences. We become more resilient, confident, and empowered to create the life we want. With a positive mindset, we can achieve our goals and realize our full potential. So, take the first step towards overcoming limiting beliefs and self-sabotage today and start living the life you want.

24: Creating a Positive Self-Image

Creating a positive self-image is essential for living a happy, fulfilling life. When we have a positive self-image, we are more confident, motivated, and resilient. We are better able to handle challenges and setbacks, and we are more likely to pursue our passions and achieve our goals. In this chapter, we will explore the ways in which we can create a positive self-image and cultivate a positive mindset.

What is a Self-Image?

Our self-image is the way we see ourselves. It is the mental image we have of ourselves, based on our experiences, beliefs, and perceptions. Our self-image can be positive or negative, and it can have a significant impact on our lives.

A positive self-image is characterized by feelings of self-worth, self-respect, and self-love. It is based on an accurate assessment of our strengths and weaknesses, and it allows us to feel confident and motivated. On the other hand, a negative self-image is characterized by feelings of self-doubt, self-criticism, and self-hatred. It can hold us back from pursuing our goals and living a fulfilling life.

Creating a Positive Self-Image

Creating a positive self-image takes time, effort, and practice. Here are some practical tips for cultivating a positive self-image:

– Practice self-compassion: Self-compassion is the act of treating yourself with kindness, understanding, and empathy. It is essential for creating a positive self-image. When we practice self-compassion, we are able to accept our flaws and mistakes and treat ourselves with the same kindness we would offer to a friend.

– Identify your strengths: Take some time to identify your strengths and celebrate them. Focus on what you do well and what you enjoy doing. When we focus on our strengths, we feel more confident and motivated.

– Challenge negative self-talk: Negative self-talk can hold us back from creating a positive self-image. Challenge your negative self-talk by asking yourself if your thoughts are based on facts or assumptions. Look for evidence that contradicts your negative thoughts and replace them with positive affirmations.

– Set realistic goals: Setting realistic goals is essential for creating a positive self-image. When we set goals that are too ambitious or unrealistic, we set ourselves up for failure. Start with small, achievable goals and build up from there.

– Take care of yourself: Taking care of yourself is essential for creating a positive self-image. Get enough sleep, eat a healthy diet, exercise regularly, and take time for self-care activities that bring you joy.

– Surround yourself with positivity: Surround yourself with positivity by spending time with people who support and encourage you. Read books and listen to podcasts that inspire and motivate you.

– Practice gratitude: Practicing gratitude is essential for creating a positive self-image. Take time each day to reflect on the things you are grateful for. When we focus on the positive aspects of our lives, we feel happier and more fulfilled.

Creating a positive self-image is essential for living a happy, fulfilling life. By practicing self-compassion, identifying your strengths, challenging negative self-talk, setting realistic goals, taking care of yourself, surrounding yourself with positivity, and practicing gratitude, you can cultivate a positive self-image and a positive mindset.

Remember that creating a positive self-image is a journey, not a destination. It takes time, effort, and practice to overcome negative patterns and cultivate a positive mindset. However, the rewards of creating a positive self-image are well worth the effort. When we have a positive self-image, we are more confident, motivated, and resilient. We are better able to handle challenges and setbacks, and we are more likely to pursue our passions and achieve our goals. So, take the first step towards creating a positive self-image today and start living the life you want. Remember that you are worthy of love and respect, and that you have the power to create the life you deserve. By cultivating a positive self-image, you can unlock your full potential and achieve your dreams.

25: Overcoming Addiction with Positive Thinking

Overcoming addiction can be a challenging and complex journey, but with the power of positive thinking, it is possible to break free from the cycle of addiction and reclaim your life. Positive thinking can help you build resilience, develop self-awareness, and cultivate a sense of purpose and meaning. In this chapter, we will explore the ways in which positive thinking can help you overcome addiction and live a fulfilling life in recovery.

What is Addiction?

Addiction is a chronic disease that affects the brain and behavior. It is characterized by compulsive drug seeking and use despite harmful consequences. Addiction can take many forms, including alcoholism, drug addiction, gambling addiction, sex addiction, and more. Addiction is often accompanied by negative emotions such as shame, guilt, and hopelessness.

How Positive Thinking Can Help Overcome Addiction

Positive thinking can help you overcome addiction in the

following ways:

– Building Resilience: Positive thinking can help you build resilience, which is the ability to bounce back from adversity. When you face challenges in recovery, positive thinking can help you stay focused on your goals and maintain a sense of hope and optimism. By cultivating a positive mindset, you can develop the resilience you need to overcome addiction and stay sober.

– Developing Self-Awareness: Positive thinking can help you develop self-awareness, which is the ability to recognize and understand your own thoughts, feelings, and behaviors. By becoming more self-aware, you can identify triggers and negative thought patterns that may lead to relapse. By practicing positive thinking, you can learn to reframe negative thoughts and emotions and develop healthier coping mechanisms.

– Cultivating Purpose and Meaning: Addiction often leaves people feeling lost and without a sense of purpose or meaning. Positive thinking can help you find purpose and meaning in recovery by focusing on your strengths, values, and goals. By cultivating a sense of purpose and meaning, you can stay motivated and committed to your recovery journey.

Tips for Using Positive Thinking in Addiction Recovery

Here are some practical tips for using positive thinking to overcome addiction:

– Practice Gratitude: Gratitude is a powerful tool for cultivating positive thinking. Take time each day to reflect on the things you are grateful for, no matter how small they may seem. Gratitude can help shift your focus from what you have lost to what you have gained in recovery.

– Practice Mindfulness: Mindfulness is the practice of being present and fully engaged in the moment. By practicing mindfulness, you can learn to accept your thoughts and emotions without judgment. This can help you develop greater self-awareness and better cope with cravings and triggers.

– Visualize Success: Visualization is the practice of imagining yourself achieving your goals. By visualizing success, you can develop a positive mindset and increase your motivation to stay sober. Imagine yourself living a happy, fulfilling life in recovery, and let that vision inspire you to keep going.

– Focus on Positive Self-Talk: Positive self-talk is the practice of using positive affirmations to challenge negative thoughts and beliefs. When you catch yourself thinking negative thoughts, reframe them in a positive way. For example, instead of thinking "I can't do this," say "I am strong enough to overcome this challenge."

– Surround Yourself with Supportive People: Surrounding yourself with supportive people is essential for staying motivated and committed to your recovery journey. Seek out people who share your goals and values, and who will support and encourage you along the way.

Overcoming addiction with positive thinking is possible. By building resilience, developing self-awareness, and cultivating a sense of purpose and meaning, you can break free from the cycle of addiction and live a fulfilling life in recovery. Remember that addiction recovery is a journey, not a destination. It takes time, effort, and support to overcome addiction and stay sober.

25: OVERCOMING ADDICTION WITH POSITIVE THINKING

If you are struggling with addiction, know that you are not alone. There are many resources available to help you on your journey, including support groups, therapy, and medication-assisted treatment. By combining these resources with the power of positive thinking, you can overcome addiction and create a brighter future for yourself.

Remember that addiction does not define you. You are a person with strengths, weaknesses, and unique qualities that make you who you are. By practicing positive thinking and embracing your true self, you can break free from the cycle of addiction and live a happy, healthy life in recovery.

26: The Role of Positive Thinking in Stress Management

Stress is a normal part of life, but when it becomes overwhelming, it can have negative effects on our physical, mental, and emotional health. In order to manage stress effectively, it is important to develop healthy coping mechanisms, including positive thinking. In this chapter, we will explore the role of positive thinking in stress management and how you can use it to improve your well-being.

What is Positive Thinking?

Positive thinking is the practice of focusing on positive thoughts and beliefs in order to improve one's mental and emotional well-being. It involves reframing negative thoughts and emotions into more positive ones, and finding reasons to be optimistic and hopeful, even in difficult situations.

The Role of Positive Thinking in Stress Management

Positive thinking can play a powerful role in managing stress. Here are some ways in which positive thinking can help you cope with stress:

26: THE ROLE OF POSITIVE THINKING IN STRESS MANAGEMENT

– Reframe Negative Thoughts: When we experience stress, our thoughts often become negative and self-critical. Positive thinking can help us reframe these thoughts into more positive and constructive ones. For example, instead of thinking "I can't handle this," we can reframe our thoughts to "I can do my best and ask for help if I need it."

– Promote Optimism: Optimism is the belief that things will work out in the end, even in the face of challenges and setbacks. Positive thinking can help promote optimism by focusing on the positive aspects of a situation and visualizing a positive outcome. This can help reduce stress and increase feelings of hope and resilience.

– Improve Resilience: Resilience is the ability to bounce back from adversity. Positive thinking can help improve resilience by promoting a growth mindset, which is the belief that we can learn and grow from our challenges. By adopting a growth mindset, we can approach stress as an opportunity for growth and learning, rather than a source of anxiety and fear.

– Boost Self-Esteem: Stress can often lead to feelings of self-doubt and low self-esteem. Positive thinking can help boost self-esteem by focusing on our strengths and accomplishments, and reframing negative self-talk into positive affirmations. This can help increase our confidence and reduce stress.

– Increase Social Support: Positive thinking can also help us build stronger social support networks. When we approach others with a positive attitude and outlook, we are more likely to receive positive responses and support. This can help us feel more connected and supported, which can in turn reduce stress.

Tips for Using Positive Thinking in Stress Management

Here are some practical tips for using positive thinking to manage stress:

– Practice Gratitude: Gratitude is a powerful tool for cultivating positive thinking. Take time each day to reflect on the things you are grateful for, no matter how small they may seem. Gratitude can help shift your focus from stress and anxiety to the positive aspects of your life.

– Visualize Success: Visualization is the practice of imagining yourself achieving your goals. By visualizing success, you can develop a positive mindset and increase your motivation to overcome stress. Imagine yourself successfully managing your stress, and let that vision inspire you to keep going.

– Practice Self-Care: Self-care is essential for managing stress. Take time each day to do something that brings you joy and relaxation, whether it's reading a book, taking a walk, or practicing yoga. Self-care can help reduce stress and improve your overall well-being.

– Focus on Positive Self-Talk: Positive self-talk is the practice of using positive affirmations to challenge negative thoughts and beliefs. When you catch yourself thinking negative thoughts, reframe them in a positive way. For example, instead of thinking "I'm not good enough," say "I am capable and deserving of love and happiness."

– Seek Support: Remember that you don't have to manage stress alone. Seek support from friends, family, or a mental health professional. Talking to someone about your stress can help you gain perspective and find new ways to cope. A supportive network can also provide encouragement and motivation to keep going, even when things get tough.

– Practice Mindfulness: Mindfulness is the practice of being present in the moment and non-judgmentally observing your thoughts and feelings. By practicing mindfulness, you can become more aware of your stress triggers and learn to respond to them in a more positive way. Mindfulness can also help you cultivate a sense of calm and relaxation, even in the midst of stress.

– Challenge Negative Beliefs: Negative beliefs about ourselves and the world around us can contribute to stress and anxiety. Challenge these beliefs by questioning their accuracy and considering more positive alternatives. For example, if you believe that you are not capable of managing stress, challenge that belief by reminding yourself of times when you have successfully coped with challenges in the past.

Positive thinking can be a powerful tool for managing stress and improving our overall well-being. By reframing negative thoughts, promoting optimism, improving resilience, boosting self-esteem, and increasing social support, we can reduce stress and build a more positive outlook on life. Remember that managing stress is a process, and it takes time and effort to develop positive thinking habits. But with practice and persistence, you can use positive thinking to overcome stress and create a happier, healthier life.

27: Overcoming Depression with Positive Thinking

Depression is a mental health condition that affects millions of people worldwide. It can be debilitating, robbing individuals of their motivation, energy, and joy in life. While medication and therapy are often used to treat depression, positive thinking can also be a powerful tool in overcoming this condition. In this chapter, we'll explore the role of positive thinking in overcoming depression and provide practical strategies for cultivating a more positive outlook on life.

Understanding Depression

Before we dive into the role of positive thinking in overcoming depression, it's important to understand this condition. Depression is characterized by persistent feelings of sadness, hopelessness, and worthlessness, as well as a loss of interest in activities that once brought pleasure. Symptoms can vary in severity, but can include fatigue, changes in appetite and sleep patterns, difficulty concentrating, and thoughts of self-harm or suicide.

Depression can be caused by a variety of factors, including

genetics, environmental factors, and life events such as trauma, loss, or major life changes. While medication and therapy can be effective treatments for depression, there are also things individuals can do to promote positive thinking and improve their mental health.

The Role of Positive Thinking in Overcoming Depression

Positive thinking can be a powerful tool in overcoming depression. When we are depressed, our thoughts tend to be negative and self-critical, which can perpetuate the cycle of depression. By actively cultivating positive thoughts and beliefs, we can shift our perspective and improve our mental health.

– Reframe Negative Thoughts: One of the keys to overcoming depression with positive thinking is to reframe negative thoughts. This means actively challenging negative self-talk and replacing it with more positive, realistic thoughts. For example, if you find yourself thinking "I'm worthless," challenge that thought by reminding yourself of your strengths and accomplishments.

– Practice Gratitude: Cultivating a sense of gratitude can

also be helpful in overcoming depression. By focusing on the things we are grateful for, we can shift our attention away from negative thoughts and promote a more positive outlook. Consider starting a gratitude journal, where you write down three things you are grateful for each day.

– Engage in Positive Activities: Depression can make it difficult to engage in activities that once brought pleasure. However, it's important to make an effort to do things that make you feel good. This could be as simple as taking a walk outside or spending time with a loved one. By engaging in positive activities, you can boost your mood and increase your sense of well-being.

– Practice Self-Care: Taking care of yourself is an important part of overcoming depression. This means getting enough sleep, eating a healthy diet, and engaging in regular exercise. It also means taking time for activities that promote relaxation and stress relief, such as meditation, yoga, or reading a good book.

– Seek Support: Overcoming depression is not something you have to do alone. Seek support from friends, family, or a mental health professional. Talking to someone about your struggles can help you gain perspective and find new ways to cope. A supportive network can also provide encouragement and motivation to keep going, even when things get tough.

Overcoming depression is a journey, and it takes time and effort to cultivate a more positive outlook on life. But by actively cultivating positive thoughts, engaging in positive activities, and seeking support, it is possible to overcome depression and create a happier, healthier life. Remember that seeking professional help is always an option, and that there is no shame in asking for support when you need it. With a commitment to positive thinking and self-care, you can overcome depression and create a brighter future for yourself.

It's also important to remember that overcoming depression with positive thinking is not a one-size-fits-all solution. What works for one person may not work for another. It's important to experiment with different strategies and find what works best for you. Don't be discouraged if it takes time to see progress – recovery from depression is a process, and it's important to be patient and kind to yourself along the way.

In addition to the strategies outlined above, there are also some additional things you can do to support your mental health and promote positive thinking. These include:

– Practice Mindfulness: Mindfulness involves paying attention to the present moment without judgment. By practicing mindfulness, you can become more aware of your thoughts and feelings and learn to observe them without getting caught up in them. This can help you develop a more positive outlook and increase your sense of well-being.

– Challenge Negative Beliefs: In addition to challenging negative thoughts, it's also important to challenge negative beliefs that may be contributing to your depression. For example, if you believe that you are unlovable, challenge that belief by reminding yourself of times when you have felt loved and supported.

– Set Realistic Goals: Setting realistic goals can help you build a sense of accomplishment and boost your self-esteem. Start small and focus on achievable goals, such as going for a walk or completing a household task. As you accomplish these goals, you can gradually increase the difficulty level.

– Practice Self-Compassion: Finally, it's important to practice self-compassion when working to overcome depression. This means treating yourself with kindness and understanding, rather than self-criticism. Recognize that depression is a difficult condition to deal with, and give yourself credit for the progress you make, no matter how small.

In conclusion, positive thinking can be a powerful tool in overcoming depression. By actively cultivating positive thoughts, engaging in positive activities, and seeking support, it is possible to overcome depression and create a happier, healthier life. Remember to be patient, experiment with different strategies, and practice self-compassion along the way. With a commitment to positive thinking and self-care, you can overcome depression and create a brighter future for yourself.

28: The Benefits of a Positive Community

Humans are social beings, and our relationships with others can have a profound impact on our mental and physical health. In particular, being part of a positive community can have many benefits, including improved mood, reduced stress, and increased feelings of belonging and social support. In this chapter, we will explore some of the ways that being part of a positive community can benefit our well-being.

– Improved Mood: Being part of a positive community can help improve our mood and overall sense of well-being. When we spend time with people who are positive and optimistic, it can be contagious, and we may find ourselves feeling happier and more positive as a result. Positive communities can also provide a sense of purpose and meaning, which can help combat feelings of loneliness and depression.

– Reduced Stress: Being part of a positive community can also help reduce stress. When we feel supported and connected to others, we may be better able to handle the stressors in our lives. Additionally, positive communities can provide opportunities for relaxation and stress relief, such as through social events or group activities.

– Increased Belonging and Social Support: Feeling like we belong and have social support is essential for our mental and physical health. Being part of a positive community can provide a sense of belonging and acceptance, which can be particularly important for those who may feel isolated or disconnected.

Additionally, positive communities can provide social support, such as through emotional support, practical assistance, and advice.

– Opportunities for Growth and Learning: Being part of a positive community can also provide opportunities for growth and learning. Positive communities may offer educational opportunities, such as workshops or classes, that can help us develop new skills and interests. Additionally, being part of a positive community can expose us to new perspectives and ideas, which can help us broaden our understanding of the world.

– Sense of Purpose and Meaning: Finally, being part of a positive community can provide a sense of purpose and meaning. When we are part of something bigger than ourselves, we may feel more motivated and inspired to make a positive impact in the world. Additionally, positive communities may offer opportunities for service and volunteerism, which can help us feel like we are making a meaningful contribution to our communities.

In conclusion, being part of a positive community can have many benefits for our well-being. By providing a sense of belonging, social support, opportunities for growth and learning, and a sense of purpose and meaning, positive communities can help us thrive and live happier, healthier lives. Whether it's through joining a community group, volunteering, or simply spending time with positive people, cultivating positive relationships and being part of a positive community is an essential part of self-care and overall well-being.

If you are looking to become part of a positive community, here are some tips to help you get started:

– Identify Your Interests: Consider what interests and hobbies you have, and look for communities that share those interests. For example, if you love yoga, you could join a yoga class or community group.

– Seek Out Opportunities: Look for opportunities to get involved in your community, such as through volunteering or attending community events. Many communities have online forums or social media groups where you can connect with others who share your interests.

– Attend Events: Attend events hosted by community organizations or groups. This can be a great way to meet new people and connect with others who share your interests.

– Be Open to New Experiences: Try new things and be open to new experiences. You never know what you might learn or who you might meet when you step outside your comfort zone.

– Build Strong Relationships: Once you've connected with others, focus on building strong relationships by being supportive, kind, and reliable. Positive relationships are built on trust and mutual respect.

Remember, building a positive community takes time and effort, but the benefits are well worth it. By being part of a positive community, you can improve your mood, reduce stress, increase your sense of belonging, and find meaning and purpose in your life.

29: Overcoming Negative Thinking Patterns

Negative thinking patterns can be a major barrier to living a fulfilling and happy life. These patterns of thinking can lead to feelings of anxiety, depression, and low self-esteem. Fortunately, there are steps you can take to overcome negative thinking patterns and develop a more positive mindset.

– Recognize Negative Thoughts: The first step in overcoming negative thinking patterns is to become aware of them. Pay attention to your thoughts and notice when they are negative. Write down these thoughts and consider how they are affecting your mood and behavior.

– Challenge Negative Thoughts: Once you've identified negative thoughts, challenge them by asking yourself if they are based on facts or assumptions. Try to view the situation from a different perspective and consider alternative explanations.

– Replace Negative Thoughts with Positive Ones: Replace negative thoughts with positive ones. Focus on positive affirmations and statements that reinforce a positive self-image. This can help you to retrain your brain to think more positively over time.

– Practice Gratitude: Practice gratitude by focusing on the good things in your life. Take time each day to write down things you are grateful for, even small things like a beautiful sunset or a delicious cup of coffee.

– Surround Yourself with Positive People: Surround yourself with positive people who uplift and support you. Avoid spending time with people who are negative or bring you down.

– Take Care of Your Physical Health: Taking care of your physical health can also help to improve your mental health. Exercise, eat a healthy diet, and get enough sleep.

– Seek Professional Help: If negative thinking patterns persist, seek professional help from a therapist or mental health professional. They can help you develop coping strategies and provide support as you work to overcome negative thinking patterns.

– Practice Mindfulness: Mindfulness involves paying attention to the present moment without judgment. It can help you to become more aware of your thoughts and feelings, and to develop a sense of calm and inner peace. Try practicing mindfulness through meditation, deep breathing, or yoga.

– Set Realistic Goals: Setting realistic goals can help you to overcome negative thinking patterns by giving you something positive to focus on. Break your goals down into manageable steps, and celebrate your progress along the way.

– Practice Self-Care: Practicing self-care is essential for maintaining a positive mindset. Take time to do things that you enjoy, such as reading a book, taking a bath, or going for a walk. Set boundaries and say no to things that drain your energy or bring you down.

– Identify Triggers: Identify triggers that lead to negative thinking patterns and try to avoid them. For example, if watching the news makes you feel anxious, limit your exposure to it.

– Focus on Solutions: Instead of dwelling on problems, focus on solutions. Look for opportunities to make positive changes in your life, and take action to make them happen.

Remember, overcoming negative thinking patterns takes

time and effort. But by focusing on positive thinking, practicing gratitude, and surrounding yourself with positive people, you can develop a more positive mindset and lead a happier, more fulfilling life.

Remember, changing negative thinking patterns takes time and effort, but it is possible. By practicing gratitude, surrounding yourself with positive people, and taking care of your physical and mental health, you can develop a more positive mindset and overcome negative thinking patterns.

30: Harnessing the Power of Positive Emotions

Positive emotions play a crucial role in our lives. They help us to feel happy, motivated, and connected to others. Positive emotions also provide a buffer against stress and negativity. When we harness the power of positive emotions, we can improve our mental health, relationships, and overall well-being.

Here are some ways to harness the power of positive emotions:

– Practice Gratitude: Gratitude is a powerful positive emotion that can help us to feel more connected to others, increase our sense of well-being, and improve our relationships. Take time each day to reflect on the things you are grateful for, and express gratitude to others.

– Cultivate Positive Relationships: Positive relationships are essential for our mental health and well-being. Spend time with people who uplift and support you, and be intentional about building positive relationships.

– Engage in Activities that Bring You Joy: Engage in activities that bring you joy and a sense of accomplishment, such as playing music, painting, or gardening. Doing things you enjoy can boost your mood and help you to feel more positive.

– Practice Mindfulness: Mindfulness involves paying attention to the present moment without judgment. Practicing mindfulness can help you to become more aware of your emotions, and to develop a sense of calm and inner peace.

– Exercise: Exercise is a powerful way to boost positive emotions. When you exercise, your brain releases endorphins, which are natural mood-boosters. Exercise can also improve your self-esteem and confidence.

– Practice Positive Self-Talk: Positive self-talk involves replacing negative thoughts with positive ones. By focusing on positive affirmations and self-talk, you can improve your self-esteem and develop a more positive outlook on life.

– Help Others: Helping others can be a powerful way to experience positive emotions. When we help others, we feel a sense of connection and purpose. Look for opportunities to help others, such as volunteering or doing something kind for a friend.

– Focus on the Good: When we focus on the good things in our lives, we can improve our mood and overall well-being. Try to focus on positive aspects of your life, even when things are challenging.

– Celebrate Your Accomplishments: Celebrating your accomplishments can help you to feel proud of yourself and boost your self-esteem. Take time to celebrate your successes, no matter how small.

– Laugh: Laughter is a powerful way to experience positive emotions. Watch a funny movie, spend time with friends who make you laugh, or engage in activities that make you smile.

Harnessing the power of positive emotions can be a powerful way to improve your mental health, relationships, and overall well-being. By practicing gratitude, engaging in activities that bring you joy, and cultivating positive relationships, you can experience more positive emotions in your life.

Additionally, focusing on positive self-talk and mindfulness can help you to develop a more positive outlook on life. When you practice positive self-talk, you are consciously choosing to replace negative thoughts with positive ones. For example, if you catch yourself thinking, "I'm not good enough," you can replace that thought with, "I am capable and worthy of success." Over time, this practice can help to rewire your brain to focus on the positive aspects of yourself and your life.

Mindfulness can also help you to develop a more positive outlook on life. When you practice mindfulness, you are paying attention to the present moment without judgment. This means you are not dwelling on past mistakes or worrying about the future, but rather focusing on the here and now. By being present in the moment, you can appreciate the positive aspects of your life, even in the midst of challenges.

It's also important to celebrate your accomplishments, no matter how small. Celebrating your successes can help you to feel proud of yourself and boost your self-esteem. This can lead to a more positive self-image, which can in turn help you to feel more positive about your life and future.

Finally, helping others can be a powerful way to experience positive emotions. When we help others, we feel a sense of connection and purpose. This can be as simple as offering a kind word or smile to a stranger, or as involved as volunteering for a cause you care about. By helping others, you are not only making a positive impact on their lives, but you are also experiencing the positive emotions that come with it.

31: The Role of Positive Thinking in Creativity

Creativity is an essential aspect of human life, and it has been a driving force behind many of the advancements in society. Whether it is in the arts, sciences, or any other field, creativity is what enables us to innovate, solve problems, and improve our lives. However, the creative process can be challenging and frustrating, and it often requires a significant amount of mental and emotional energy. This is where positive thinking can play a crucial role in creativity.

Positive thinking refers to the practice of focusing on the positive aspects of a situation or experience, rather than dwelling on the negative. It involves cultivating a positive mindset, which can help individuals approach challenges with a more open and optimistic outlook. When it comes to creativity, positive thinking can have several benefits.

Firstly, positive thinking can help individuals overcome creative blocks. Creative blocks are a common challenge for artists, writers, musicians, and other creative professionals. They can be caused by a variety of factors, including fear, self-doubt, or lack of inspiration. When an individual is faced with a creative block, it can be easy to become frustrated or discouraged, which can further exacerbate the problem. However, by focusing on the positive aspects of the situation, such as previous successes, strengths, and opportunities, individuals can approach the challenge with a more hopeful and motivated mindset. This can help them to overcome their creative blocks and find new inspiration.

Secondly, positive thinking can help individuals take risks and explore new ideas. Creativity often requires individuals to step outside of their comfort zones and try new things. However, taking risks can be scary and intimidating, especially if an individual is prone to negative thinking. By cultivating a positive mindset, individuals can approach these new experiences with a sense of curiosity and excitement, rather than fear and hesitation. This can help them to push past their fears and explore new creative possibilities.

Thirdly, positive thinking can help individuals maintain a sense of resilience and perseverance in the face of challenges. The creative process can be unpredictable, and there are often setbacks and obstacles along the way. These challenges can be demotivating and disheartening, especially if an individual is already prone to negative thinking. However, by focusing on the positive aspects of the situation, such as learning opportunities or the progress made so far, individuals can maintain a sense of resilience and perseverance. This can help them to stay motivated and continue to work towards their creative goals, even in the face of adversity.

In addition to these benefits, positive thinking can also have a range of other positive effects on mental and emotional wellbeing. For example, studies have shown that positive thinking can improve mood, reduce stress levels, and enhance overall psychological resilience. All of these factors can contribute to a more conducive environment for creativity.

It is worth noting that positive thinking alone is not enough to guarantee creative success. Creativity requires hard work, dedication, and a willingness to take risks and learn from failures. However, positive thinking can be an essential ingredient in the creative process, helping individuals to overcome obstacles, take risks, and maintain motivation and resilience in the face of challenges.

In conclusion, positive thinking plays a vital role in creativity. By cultivating a positive mindset, individuals can overcome creative blocks, take risks, and maintain resilience in the face of challenges. Additionally, positive thinking can have a range of other positive effects on mental and emotional wellbeing, which can further enhance creativity. Therefore, it is essential to prioritize positive thinking as part of the creative process, and to work to cultivate a positive mindset that enables creative success.

There are several strategies that individuals can use to cultivate a more positive mindset and harness the power of positive thinking in creativity. One effective strategy is to practice gratitude regularly. Gratitude involves focusing on the positive aspects of one's life, rather than dwelling on the negative. By focusing on the things that one is grateful for, individuals can cultivate a more positive outlook and approach challenges with a more optimistic mindset.

Another strategy is to reframe negative thoughts into more positive ones. This involves actively challenging negative thoughts and replacing them with more positive, empowering ones. For example, instead of thinking "I can't do this," one could reframe the thought to "I am capable of learning and improving." This strategy can help individuals to break free from negative thought patterns and approach challenges with a more positive, growth-oriented mindset.

Additionally, individuals can work on building a strong support network of positive, like-minded individuals. Having a supportive community can help individuals to stay motivated, overcome creative blocks, and maintain a positive mindset, even in the face of challenges.

Finally, incorporating mindfulness practices, such as meditation or deep breathing, into one's daily routine can help to reduce stress and cultivate a more positive mindset. Mindfulness involves focusing on the present moment, without judgment or distraction. By incorporating mindfulness practices into one's daily routine, individuals can train their minds to stay present and focused, rather than getting caught up in negative thoughts or worries about the future.

In conclusion, positive thinking is a powerful tool for creativity. By cultivating a more positive mindset, individuals can overcome creative blocks, take risks, and maintain resilience in the face of challenges. Strategies such as gratitude, reframing negative thoughts, building a strong support network, and incorporating mindfulness practices into one's daily routine can all help to cultivate a more positive mindset and harness the power of positive thinking in creativity.

32: Overcoming Self-Doubt with Positive Thinking

Self-doubt is a common challenge that many people face, especially when it comes to pursuing their goals and dreams. It is a feeling of uncertainty or lack of confidence in oneself, and it can be a significant obstacle to success. However, overcoming self-doubt is possible, and positive thinking can be a powerful tool in this process.

Positive thinking involves focusing on the positive aspects of a situation or experience, rather than dwelling on the negative. It involves cultivating a positive mindset, which can help individuals approach challenges with a more open and optimistic outlook. When it comes to overcoming self-doubt, positive thinking can have several benefits.

Firstly, positive thinking can help individuals to challenge negative thoughts and beliefs about themselves. Self-doubt often stems from negative self-talk, such as "I'm not good enough," or "I'll never be able to do this." These thoughts can be demotivating and hold individuals back from pursuing their goals. However, by focusing on the positive aspects of themselves, such as their strengths, accomplishments, and unique qualities, individuals can challenge these negative thoughts and build a more positive self-image.

Secondly, positive thinking can help individuals to take action and move towards their goals, even in the face of self-doubt. Self-doubt can be paralyzing, and it can prevent individuals from taking action towards their goals. However, by focusing on the positive aspects of the situation, such as the potential rewards of pursuing their goals or the progress they have already made, individuals can motivate themselves to take action, even when self-doubt is present.

Thirdly, positive thinking can help individuals to bounce back from setbacks and failures. Self-doubt can be particularly challenging when faced with setbacks or failures. It can be easy to get caught up in negative thoughts and give up on pursuing one's goals. However, by focusing on the positive aspects of the situation, such as the lessons learned or the potential for growth and improvement, individuals can bounce back from setbacks and use them as opportunities for growth and learning.

In addition to these benefits, positive thinking can also have a range of other positive effects on mental and emotional wellbeing. For example, studies have shown that positive thinking can improve mood, reduce stress levels, and enhance overall psychological resilience. All of these factors can contribute to a more conducive environment for overcoming self-doubt and pursuing one's goals.

It is worth noting that positive thinking alone is not enough to overcome self-doubt completely. Overcoming self-doubt requires hard work, dedication, and a willingness to challenge negative thoughts and beliefs about oneself. However, positive thinking can be an essential ingredient in this process, helping individuals to challenge negative thoughts, take action towards their goals, and bounce back from setbacks and failures.

There are several strategies that individuals can use to cultivate a more positive mindset and harness the power of positive thinking in overcoming self-doubt. One effective strategy is to practice self-compassion regularly. Self-compassion involves treating oneself with kindness and understanding, rather than harsh self-judgment. By practicing self-compassion, individuals can build a more positive self-image and cultivate a more forgiving and understanding attitude towards themselves.

32: OVERCOMING SELF-DOUBT WITH POSITIVE THINKING

Another strategy is to set achievable goals and celebrate small wins along the way. Setting achievable goals and celebrating small wins can help individuals build momentum towards their larger goals and feel a sense of accomplishment along the way. This can help to build confidence and challenge self-doubt.

Additionally, individuals can work on building a strong support network of positive, like-minded individuals. Having a supportive community can help individuals to stay motivated, overcome self-doubt, and maintain a positive mindset, even in the face of challenges.

Finally, incorporating mindfulness practices, such as meditation or deep breathing, into one's daily routine can also help to reduce stress and cultivate a more positive mindset. Mindfulness involves focusing on the present moment, without judgment or distraction. By incorporating mindfulness practices into one's daily routine, individuals can train their minds to stay present and focused, rather than getting caught up in negative thoughts or worries about the future.

In conclusion, self-doubt can be a significant obstacle to success, but it is possible to overcome with the help of positive thinking. Positive thinking can help individuals to challenge negative thoughts and beliefs, take action towards their goals, and bounce back from setbacks and failures. Strategies such as practicing self-compassion, setting achievable goals, building a strong support network, and incorporating mindfulness practices into one's daily routine can all help to cultivate a more positive mindset and overcome self-doubt. It is important to remember that overcoming self-doubt takes time and effort, but with the help of positive thinking, it is possible to build a more confident and resilient self-image and pursue one's goals with greater success.

33: The Impact of Positive Thinking on Leadership

Positive thinking can have a significant impact on leadership, both in terms of the leader's personal effectiveness and the effectiveness of the team or organization they are leading. A leader who cultivates a positive mindset can inspire their team, build trust and collaboration, and navigate challenges with resilience and creativity.

Here are some ways in which positive thinking can impact leadership:

– Inspires and motivates the team: A leader who maintains a positive outlook can inspire and motivate their team members to achieve their goals. When leaders focus on the positive aspects of the situation and communicate this to their team, it can create a sense of optimism and enthusiasm that motivates team members to work towards a shared vision.

– Builds trust and collaboration: A leader who approaches challenges with a positive mindset can build trust and collaboration within their team. Positive thinking can help leaders to communicate effectively and listen actively, which can foster a sense of trust and collaboration among team members. This can lead to greater creativity, innovation, and productivity.

– Enhances resilience: A leader who practices positive thinking can enhance their resilience and that of their team. When faced with challenges, leaders who approach the situation with a positive mindset can identify opportunities for growth and learning. This can help them and their team to bounce back from setbacks and failures and find new solutions to old problems.

– Encourages creativity and innovation: A leader who fosters a positive mindset can encourage creativity and innovation in their team. Positive thinking can help leaders to view challenges as opportunities for growth and experimentation, rather than as obstacles to be avoided. This can lead to greater creativity and innovation in problem-solving and decision-making.

– Improves communication: A leader who practices positive thinking can improve their communication skills. Positive thinking can help leaders to approach communication with a solution-oriented mindset. This can lead to clearer and

more effective communication, which can reduce misunderstandings and conflicts within the team.

– Builds a positive organizational culture: A leader who cultivates a positive mindset can help to build a positive organizational culture. When leaders focus on the positive aspects
of their team members and the organization as a whole, it
can create a sense of shared purpose and a positive working
environment. This can lead to greater employee satisfaction, engagement, and retention.

To cultivate a more positive mindset, leaders can take several steps, including:

– Practicing gratitude: Gratitude is an essential component
of positive thinking. Leaders can start each day by reflecting
on the things they are grateful for, whether it be the support
of their team members, the opportunity to lead, or the progress they have made towards their goals.

– Focusing on strengths: Leaders can focus on their
strengths and the strengths of their team members. By focusing on strengths, leaders can build a more positive and
confident self-image and empower their team members to

leverage their strengths to achieve their goals.

– Challenging negative thoughts: Leaders can challenge negative thoughts and beliefs about themselves and their team members. By questioning negative self-talk and reframing it in a positive light, leaders can build a more positive and solution-oriented mindset.

– Communicating positively: Leaders can communicate positively with their team members. By focusing on the positive aspects of the situation, leaders can inspire and motivate their team members, reduce misunderstandings and conflicts, and create a more positive working environment.

In conclusion, positive thinking can have a significant impact on leadership. Leaders who cultivate a positive mindset can inspire their team, build trust and collaboration, enhance resilience, encourage creativity and innovation, improve communication, and build a positive organizational culture. By taking steps to cultivate a more positive mindset, leaders can enhance their personal effectiveness and the effectiveness of their team or organization.

Additionally, a leader who practices positive thinking can

also create a culture of psychological safety within their team. Psychological safety refers to a sense of trust and respect within a team, where team members feel comfortable expressing their opinions, ideas, and concerns without fear of negative consequences. When a leader practices positive thinking, they can create an environment where team members feel valued and appreciated, which can increase their confidence and sense of belonging within the team. This, in turn, can lead to greater collaboration, innovation, and creativity.

Furthermore, positive thinking can also improve a leader's decision-making skills. When a leader approaches a decision with a positive mindset, they are more likely to see the potential opportunities and benefits of different options. They are also more likely to consider the perspectives of different team members and stakeholders, leading to more informed and inclusive decisions. This can enhance the overall performance and success of the team or organization.

However, it is important to note that positive thinking alone is not enough to be an effective leader. Leaders must also possess other key qualities, such as strong communication skills, emotional intelligence, and the ability to inspire and motivate others. Positive thinking can complement these qualities, but it cannot replace them.

In conclusion, positive thinking can have a significant impact on leadership by inspiring and motivating the team, building trust and collaboration, enhancing resilience, encouraging creativity and innovation, improving communication, and building a positive organizational culture. By taking steps to cultivate a more positive mindset, leaders can enhance their personal effectiveness and the effectiveness of their team or organization. Ultimately, positive thinking is an essential tool for leaders who want to inspire their team members, navigate challenges with creativity and resilience, and achieve their goals with greater success.

34: Positive Thinking and Spiritual Growth

Positive thinking and spiritual growth are closely related, as both involve cultivating a positive and optimistic mindset, developing inner peace, and focusing on personal growth and transformation. In this chapter, we will explore the relationship between positive thinking and spiritual growth, and how they can work together to promote greater happiness, fulfillment, and wellbeing.

Spiritual growth is a process of inner transformation that involves developing a deeper connection with oneself, others, and the divine. It is about discovering our true purpose in life and living in alignment with our values and beliefs. Positive thinking is a key component of spiritual growth, as it involves focusing on the positive aspects of life and cultivating a sense of gratitude, optimism, and hope.

Here are some ways in which positive thinking can promote spiritual growth:

– Cultivating a sense of gratitude: Gratitude is an essential component of positive thinking and spiritual growth. When we focus on the things we are grateful for, we cultivate a sense of appreciation for the blessings in our lives. This can help us to develop a deeper sense of connection with the divine and with others, and to live in a more compassionate and loving way.

– Developing inner peace: Positive thinking can help us to develop inner peace by reducing the negative thoughts and emotions that cause us to feel stressed, anxious, or overwhelmed. When we cultivate a positive and optimistic mindset, we can find greater calmness and clarity in our daily lives, which can help us to connect more deeply with our inner selves and with the divine.

– Living in alignment with our values: Positive thinking can help us to live in alignment with our values and beliefs. When we focus on the positive aspects of life, we can see how our actions and behaviors are connected to our values, and we can make choices that are in line with our highest aspirations. This can help us to live a more purposeful and meaningful life.

– Fostering a sense of connection: Positive thinking can help us to foster a sense of connection with others and with the divine. When we focus on the positive aspects of life, we can see how we are all interconnected and how our actions and thoughts can impact others. This can help us to develop greater compassion and empathy for others and to live in a more loving and harmonious way.

– Embracing personal growth and transformation: Positive thinking can help us to embrace personal growth and transformation by seeing challenges as opportunities for learning and growth. When we approach life with a positive and optimistic mindset, we can see how our experiences are helping us to become the best version of ourselves. This can help us to live a more fulfilling and purposeful life.

To cultivate positive thinking for spiritual growth, we can take several steps, including:

– Practicing gratitude: We can practice gratitude by taking time each day to reflect on the things we are grateful for, whether it be the people in our lives, the experiences we have had, or the opportunities we have been given.

– Mindfulness meditation: Mindfulness meditation involves focusing on the present moment, without judgment or distraction. This can help us to develop greater awareness of our thoughts and emotions, and to cultivate a more positive and compassionate mindset.

– Affirmations: Affirmations involve repeating positive statements to ourselves, such as "I am worthy and deserving of love and happiness." This can help us to reprogram our subconscious mind with positive beliefs and to cultivate a more positive and confident self-image.

– Reading spiritual texts: Reading spiritual texts can help us to develop a deeper understanding of our connection to the divine and to others. This can inspire us to live in a more loving, compassionate, and purposeful way.

– Practicing forgiveness: Forgiveness involves letting go of negative emotions and resentments towards others. When we practice forgiveness, we can cultivate a more positive and compassionate mindset, and develop a deeper sense of connection with others.

– Surrounding ourselves with positive influences: We can surround ourselves with positive people, books, music, and other sources of inspiration to help us cultivate a more positive mindset and foster spiritual growth.

– Serving others: Serving others can help us to develop

greater compassion and empathy, and to cultivate a more positive and loving mindset. When we serve others, we are reminded of our interconnectedness and can find greater meaning and purpose in our lives.

Positive thinking and spiritual growth can work together to help us live a more fulfilling and purposeful life. By cultivating a positive and optimistic mindset, we can develop greater inner peace, connection with others, and alignment with our values and beliefs. This can help us to become the best version of ourselves, and to make a positive impact in the world around us.

35: Creating a Personalized Positive Thinking Plan

Creating a personalized positive thinking plan can be an effective way to cultivate a more positive and optimistic mindset, and to improve your overall wellbeing. By developing a plan that is tailored to your unique needs and goals, you can create a roadmap for success and achieve greater happiness, fulfillment, and success in your personal and professional life. In this chapter, we will explore how to create a personalized positive thinking plan, including the key steps and strategies you can use to achieve your goals.

Step 1: Identify Your Goals

The first step in creating a personalized positive thinking plan is to identify your goals. What do you want to achieve through positive thinking? What areas of your life do you want to improve? Examples of goals might include reducing stress, improving your self-confidence, or cultivating greater gratitude.

Once you have identified your goals, it is important to be specific and measurable. For example, instead of saying "I want to reduce stress," you might say "I want to reduce my stress levels by 50% within the next three months."

Step 2: Identify Your Strengths and Weaknesses

The next step in creating a personalized positive thinking plan is to identify your strengths and weaknesses. This can help you to identify areas where you need to focus your efforts, and areas where you can leverage your existing strengths to achieve your goals.

For example, if you are naturally optimistic and have a positive attitude, you might focus on cultivating greater gratitude and mindfulness. If you struggle with self-doubt and negative self-talk, you might focus on developing greater self-compassion and confidence.

Step 3: Develop a Positive Thinking Strategy

The next step is to develop a positive thinking strategy that is tailored to your goals, strengths, and weaknesses. This might include a combination of techniques and strategies, such as:

– Affirmations: Affirmations are positive statements that you repeat to yourself to help reprogram your subconscious mind with positive beliefs. For example, "I am worthy and deserving of success and happiness."

– Visualization: Visualization involves imagining yourself achieving your goals and experiencing positive outcomes. This can help you to create a sense of motivation and inspiration, and to build greater confidence and belief in your ability to succeed.

– Gratitude: Gratitude involves focusing on the positive aspects of your life and cultivating a sense of appreciation for the blessings in your life. This can help you to develop greater resilience, optimism, and wellbeing.

– Mindfulness: Mindfulness involves focusing on the present moment, without judgment or distraction. This can help you to develop greater awareness of your thoughts and emotions, and to cultivate a more positive and compassionate mindset.

– Positive Self-Talk: Positive self-talk involves consciously replacing negative self-talk with positive affirmations and beliefs. This can help you to develop greater self-confidence and self-compassion, and to overcome self-doubt and negativity.

Step 4: Implement Your Plan

The final step in creating a personalized positive thinking plan is to implement your plan and track your progress. This might involve setting weekly or monthly goals, tracking your progress using a journal or app, and making adjustments to your plan as needed.

It is also important to be patient and consistent in your efforts. Positive thinking is a habit that requires ongoing practice and dedication, and it may take time to see results. However, by staying committed to your plan and focusing on your goals, you can achieve greater happiness, fulfillment, and success in your life.

In conclusion, creating a personalized positive thinking plan can be an effective way to cultivate a more positive and optimistic mindset, and to improve your overall wellbeing. By identifying your goals, strengths, and weaknesses, and developing a positive thinking strategy that is tailored to your unique needs, you can create a roadmap for success and achieve your goals. With patience, consistency, and dedication, you can develop a more positive and fulfilling life that aligns with your values and aspirations. Remember to celebrate your successes along the way, and to stay focused on your goals even when faced with challenges or setbacks. With a personalized positive thinking plan, you can achieve greater happiness, resilience, and success in all areas of your life.

36: Conclusion: Living Your Best Life with Positive Thinking

In conclusion, positive thinking is a powerful tool that can help us to live our best lives, both personally and professionally. By cultivating a positive and optimistic mindset, we can improve our overall wellbeing, achieve greater success and fulfillment, and make a positive impact in the world around us.

Throughout this guide, we have explored the many benefits of positive thinking, including improved mental and physical health, greater resilience and adaptability, enhanced creativity and problem-solving skills, and stronger relationships and connections with others. We have also discussed some of the key strategies and techniques that we can use to cultivate a more positive mindset, including developing self-awareness, practicing mindfulness and gratitude, surrounding ourselves with positive influences, and engaging in regular exercise and self-care.

However, it is important to remember that positive thinking is not a cure-all or a magic solution. Life is full of challenges and setbacks, and it is natural to experience negative emotions and thoughts from time to time. The key is to use positive thinking as a tool to help us navigate these challenges and overcome obstacles, rather than as a way to avoid or suppress difficult emotions.

Living your best life with positive thinking requires ongoing effort, commitment, and dedication. It requires us to be intentional about our thoughts and beliefs, and to make conscious choices that align with our values and aspirations. It also requires us to be patient and compassionate with ourselves, and to recognize that growth and progress are often gradual and incremental.

Ultimately, the power of positive thinking lies in our ability to shape our own experiences and perspectives. By choosing to focus on the positive aspects of our lives, we can create a more fulfilling and meaningful existence, one that is aligned with our deepest values and aspirations. So, whether you are facing a challenging situation or simply seeking to improve your overall wellbeing, remember that the power of positive thinking is within you. By cultivating a more positive and optimistic mindset, you can live your best life and create a better world for yourself and those around you.

It is also important to note that positive thinking does not mean that we ignore or deny negative emotions or situations. It is important to acknowledge and process difficult emotions, and to take steps to address challenging situations. However, with a positive and optimistic mindset, we can approach these challenges with greater resilience, creativity, and determination.

In addition, it is important to remember that positive thinking is not a one-size-fits-all solution. What works for one person may not work for another, and it is important to find the strategies and techniques that resonate with us personally. This may involve trying out different approaches and experimenting with different techniques until we find what works best for us.

Finally, it is important to recognize that positive thinking is not a destination, but rather a journey. It is an ongoing process of growth, learning, and self-discovery. We may experience setbacks and challenges along the way, but with a positive and resilient mindset, we can overcome these obstacles and continue to grow and develop.

In conclusion, living your best life with positive thinking requires effort, commitment, and dedication. It requires us to be intentional about our thoughts and beliefs, and to make conscious choices that align with our values and aspirations. It also requires us to be patient and compassionate with ourselves, and to recognize that growth and progress are often gradual and incremental. By cultivating a more positive and optimistic mindset, we can create a more fulfilling and meaningful existence, one that is aligned with our deepest values and aspirations. So, whether you are facing a challenging situation or simply seeking to improve your overall wellbeing, remember that the power of positive thinking is within you.

Thank You

As we reach the end of this book, I want to say thanks for reading this book.

I want to get this information out to as many people as possible. If you found this book helpful, I would greatly appreciate you leaving me a review. This helps others find the book as well.

Disclaimer

This document is geared towards providing exact and reliable information in regards to the topic and issue covered. The publication is sold on the idea that the publisher is not required to render an accounting, officially permitted, or otherwise, qualified services. If advice is necessary, legal, financial, medical or professional, a practiced individual in the profession should be ordered.

This information is not presented by a financial or medical practitioner and is for entertainment, educational and informational purposes only. The content is not intended as a substitute for professional medical advice, diagnosis, or treatment. Always seek the advice of your physician or other qualified health care provider with any questions you may have regarding a medical condition. Never disregard professional medical advice or delay in seeking it because of something you have read.

The information provided herein is stated to be truthful and consistent, in that any liability, in terms of inattention or otherwise, by any usage or abuse of any policies, processes, or directions contained within is the solitary and utter responsibility of the recipient reader. Under no circumstances

DISCLAIMER

will any legal responsibility or blame be held against the publisher for any reparation, damages, or monetary loss due to the information herein, either directly or indirectly.

www.ingramcontent.com/pod-product-compliance
Lightning Source LLC
Chambersburg PA
CBHW060518130626

46553CB00002B/554